TWO-PART INVENTIONS

BOOKS BY
RICHARD HOWARD

POETRY
Two-Part Inventions   *1974*
Findings   *1971*
Untitled Subjects   *1969*
The Damages   *1967*
Quantities   *1962*

CRITICISM
Alone with America   *1969*

CRITICAL ANTHOLOGY
(PHOTOGRAPHS BY TOM VICTOR)
Preferences   *1974*

TWO-PART INVENTIONS

POEMS BY

RICHARD HOWARD

Atheneum NEW YORK *1974*

The poems have been previously published as follows:

AFTER THE FACTS: *Horizon*
WILD FLOWERS: *New American Review*
A PHENOMENON OF NATURE: *Poetry*
THE LESSON OF THE MASTER: *Shenandoah*
A NATURAL DEATH: *Craft Horizons*

For KATHLEEN *and* HARRY FORD

... wherein the lovers of the instrument are shown a way to play clearly in two voices and ... to arrive at a singing style and at the same time to acquire a strong foretaste of composition. J. S. BACH

Contents

TWO-PART INVENTIONS

AFTER THE FACTS

Johann Christian Friedrich Hölderlin, 1770-1843

I

Villandry, "Les Douves" par Azay-le-Rideau,
December 28, 1822.
My dear M. Prüfe, do you not recall,
      in reply to yours,
a letter from the late Louis Destourd,
Mayor of Villandry, Deputy from Blois?
I myself recall it, though I never saw
      the text at the time,
for it has become the sad (though inspiring)
duty of his only daughter to dispose
of the lamented M. Destourd's effects,
      among which I find,
with some emotion, your inquiry preserved.
To that, as to any sollicitation,
his answers were doubtless satisfactory,
      as far as they go,
yet my father left no orders that the case,
by the mere occasion of *his* rejoinder,
must be judged—say, by his daughter—to be *closed.*
      Therefore I resume—
though responsibility, even were he
alive, would no longer be Papa's *alone,*
for since the period of your interest
      I have myself turned
wife and mother, thrice over: need I remark,
it is my *maternity* which has tripled!
I remain married, with a felicity
      to which I believe
that of my sons attests, to the *same husband,*
Henri Fourières, a fervent patron of the arts,

indeed a perfect virtuoso upon
        the *arpeggione,*
and it is consonant with his character,
as with his accomplishments, that he spurs me
to speak of the events of long years ago
        (before our marriage),
regarding which you wrote so purposefully
to poor Papa. It has occurred to *me*, as well,
that my narrative, my impressions, my words
        may be of some use
in restoring to his proper genius
a poet, as you intimated, forlorn
in the prime of his prophetic mission.
        Mad or even masked
as "Scardanelli" (the one clue you afford),
I would succor a man who discards his own
identity—let me describe to you more
        circumstantially
than Papa ever could or *would* (my father
was the son, necessarily, of another age—
an age perhaps of clearer vision, clearly
        one of drier eyes),
more *flagrantly*, as Papa would have phrased it,
the Episode I figured in to such effect.
Discover to your mysterious "patient"
        my recollections,
for one memory makes us all remember,
and I am certain what so amazed me, then,
is with him, now, wherere his mind may be.
        I have plagued *my* wits
to "place" the man—between your Schiller and your
Schlegel, though surely neither: too young, too fair,
yet the eminence you intimate was there.
        Will you not name him?
It had been one of those autumn afternoons,
ageless, unswept, apparently infinite—
weather which to reminiscence seems a rule
        of life in those days.
At first I scarcely glanced up from the volume
(the Cérieux edition, I have it still,
of Sénancour's romance, or is it nonsense
        so to qualify
a work of such laborious melancholy?) ...

As I say, I was not inclined to leave off
reading to Papa, for I supposed the sound
   no more than the cry
of our peacocks, more strident at that season,
in fine weather. How like my father it was,
to cultivate the white variety alone
   and fondly insist
the creatures supplied by harshness of accent
what they lacked in luster! Granting it was so,
the present intonation was too gentle,
   too *lamentable*
to be the clamor of our particular birds,
and I suspect a sort of curiosity
conquered my reluctance to lay by the tale
   of poor *Obermann.*
So I stood up (in white muslin, sprigged, white silk
ribbons on my straw bonnet, white string gloves, too
—white was my color then, all in white, and one
   crimson cabbage-rose),
took Papa's arm, and with him passed down the steps
of our terrace to the great basin below,
advancing with some concern, as I have said,
   but no real alarm.
There, uttering at intervals the eery
ululation I have just alluded to,
then falling silent, though the fountain guttered
   a grief of its own,
there, beyond the basin, stood, or stooped, or knelt
—I cannot through the curtain of forced water,
as through the fabric of Time itself, be sure
   of the man's posture—
a sad and shabby Stranger who showed, when we
circled the margin and ventured to approach,
by the misery of his apparel as by
   the mist in his eyes,
that he was none of our neighbors, nor indeed
an inhibitant of our nation. With no
surprise, no deference, no vestige even
   of obsequity
in his demeanor, the Wanderer addressed
himself to my father, though his gaze was fixed
on me, as if I were some white misgiving
   in his darkened mind.

I shall never, I know, forget what he said—
though I must break off, my dear M. Prüfe,
before I have fairly begun, in order
        to bring you the scene
in all its *enchantment* (the one word to choose) :
our basin was quite embowered by a whole
people of Grecian gods, marbles we had bought
        from "the Canova
of Blois," Théophile Clore. In pale attitudes
of power they ringed the pool, figures white
against the dingy water where the Stranger
        knelt (I see that, now—
had I dropped my rose ?) ensorcelled as we came
upon him—it was like a play ! knelt before
the statue of Pomona, I think, gasping :
        "It is Aglaia !
But the water should be brighter, like the Spring
of Erechtheus. It is unworthy of the gods
to see their images in a dark mirror.
        But we are not—" this
with a terrible sigh, "we are not in Greece."
"Are you then a Greek ?" asked Papa, gesturing,
"and are these your gods ?" "These ? Neither mine nor yours.
        We have come too late
for them. It is the world which is divine now,
and that is why there is no God. The divine
has no name, only the gods are named, like these,
        and they change their names."
My father was a man of principle, not
a man of faith, and would have pursued the point
(it is no common thing, to hold such discourse
        with a Wanderer
in one's park), yet even as he made to speak,
the ragged man rushed on : "To be what we are—
that is to be divine. But the gods are dead,
        the world is alone,
and knowledge—knowledge . . ." here he fixed upon me
eyes that seemed to draw my own into a pool
of dim oblivion, "knowledge is only
        knowledge of our death."
By these words it was apparent, to Papa,
the speaker was a German ; he asked his name.

6

Thereupon the man fell again to his knees,
              his face in his hands
(which I had occasion then to remark: thin,
pale for all the dirt, and curving at the tips
as if they would scoop the darkness hovering
              round the blue pupils)
and promised to tell us . . . the next day!   "It is
difficult for me, remembering my name.
To escape a city is one thing, to choose
              a road, another."
These were his last words, for with them, as if
summoned *by* them, one of our peacocks appeared,
crest trembling like a lyre, coral claws oddly
              raw upon the moss,
and with the hollow clash of an opening
parasol, spread his perfect fan before me,
white quills quivering, each one an inducement
              to admiration.
Faced with this . . . rival, the Stranger turned away,
and I never saw him again. Nor have I
forgotten what I *heard:* that night I wakened
              to a horrid scream,
never explained, from the servants' hall, a scream
like the peacocks' (though they do not cry at night).
Papa, next day, said the lunatic had fled,
              but in my own mind
I cannot yet reconcile that Wanderer
saying "the gods are dead, the world is alone"
with the howling of the night, if that was he.
              "He"—I mean the one
you desired my father to identify,
though with no more designation who he was
than the calling of Poet. *Will you not name him?*
              Nor have I yet solved
the riddle of his departure, the gaze
he gave me (that I gave him back)—then nothing
but a shriek at midnight, and the man was gone.
              Almost, I incline
to call it jealousy of a white peacock
paying court to a white girl. What is the use
of trying to fit the two visions together?
              All of us have been
children though we may not know what we knew then,

from the brink of prurience, of prying
at best, nor can you have a conception,
when you speak of his pale hands, his blue eyes,
even of his responses to questions!
what it means to minister to this man.
If he could ever regain acquaintance
with what he had spoken upon the edge
of darkness, from whose fall our dimensions
rise, then indeed might some resumption come.
The Cup, the Poem, the Light are all drunk
in darkness—how else could they be taken?
But we are beyond the edge, the margin
where you and your father met a Stranger
who may or may not have been my patient.
I read him out those portions of your tale
in which his own grievous utterances
were given. Nothing availed. With a burst
of derisive laughter, he who had once
been Master of our German Muse, who had
dedicated his odes to Schiller and
his versions of Sophocles to Hegel—
this man, my dear lady, closed his eyelids
(reddened now by nights of staring dullness)
and murmured but one phrase, so utterly
belied by his own condition (as by
his Italian comedy) that it dismays me
in the mere report: "la perfezione
è senza lamento." The rest dithered
away into incoherence. Perhaps
my little experiment did no harm—
surely it did no good. Nothing changes,
all is changed. I am obliged, nonetheless,
for your telling of an episode to which
you bring the talents of a telling pen,
indeed. Your narrative shall be added
to a memorial volume the Friends of
the Poet are compiling in witness
to his life among us. What the witless
Scardanelli makes of these matters
is no matter. You have had, dear Madame,
a privileged or a preposterous
meeting—the risk of your choice remains
with you. Though futile to its possible

subject—or object, as he must now be called—
its record is of consequence, and I am,
as I was to the late M. Destourd,
your debtor, faithfully, JOACHIM PRÜFE.

WILDFLOWERS

for Joseph Cady

Camden, 1882

Is it raining, Mary, can you see?
I hear rain. Is the road black, is it shining?
                    Dark, I can see for myself.
Put on my red tie,
        red has life in it—most men I know
dress like undertakers making sure they look
                    mournful enough to manage
their own funerals.
        No accounting for taste : we should be
grateful for that. Help me get to the window,
                    I want to see Mickle Street.
Don't you hear it now,
        something like rain, off in the distance?
My ear, maybe, is playing me tricks again ;
                    there was a rushing, like rain
when it moves closer
        and starts a millstream in the trees. No?
I guess my senses must be losing their touch.
                    It was nothing, then, nothing
more than a tantrum
        of the boneyard : best for me to hold
still in this chair and listen to my beard grow.
                    Now if hair was poetry,
then your Walt Whitman
        would be a great success. I wear out
trying to come to terms with the wrong weather—
                    what you might call *speaking terms.*
I don't want to talk
        to much else. You tell them to go home,
Mary, no visitors today—or one, just one :
                    what else is a red tie for?

Some English poet
    keeps me up, coming all the way here
from California, Colorado—coming
        to ask the usual questions.
I don't like questions
    that require answers: English questions.
That's a country of things answered. London is
        a city of things done with.
Brooklyn is different,
    New Orleans, Washington—they're my cities
of romance, all the cities of things begun.
        I may have been deliberate,
even laborious,
    but I never looked for finish. Here,
where's his name? Bucke wrote about him after
        hearing one of his lectures.
I had it somewhere.
    You let him in, Mary: no one else,
no one . . . I'm slipping—here it is, here's the name!—
        slowly, maybe, but slipping.
Who can say he has
    hold of what might be called a standing?
That's what they *do* say, though, all these visitors—
        they write, they call, and they *stay:*
it makes a problem.
    Doctor says: bar them. I can't. I won't.
Still, they bother me. One young fellow walks in,
        says, "Walt, I should like to
read you my epic
    and have your opinion of its worth."
"Thank you," say I, "but I've been paralyzed once
        already." Suppose someone
took it in his head
    to come and sit here and say nothing!
someone who knows even the first syllables
        of the great speech of silence . . .
Today's visitor,
    maybe, will mind his tongue, maybe spare you
the trouble of putting his latest tribute
        on the shelf with all the rest.
Give me enemies
    rather than these *disciples* of mine.

13

Best thing I ever heard of Browning is how
                he disapproves of all those
Societies. Not
      that I quote Browning, or care for him,
or read him : I've tried Browning on every way,
              but he don't fit. Tennyson—
now he has his place,
      a local English place : I don't see
how the world could make much use of him elsewhere—
              but the others : I conclude
most literature
      was written on all fours, and the rest
on stilts !
            ... There, Mary, the bell, I *did* hear that !
          I know my own bell, don't I ?
Go on, go on down,
      bring the man up . . .
          In here, Mr. Wilde.
This room is not such a ruin as it seems :
         I find most things I search for
without much trouble—
      found Dr. Bucke's letter with your
name, for instance. Found my red necktie as well.
         Come in, you cast a shadow
where you stand. Come in,
      the chaos is more suspected than real.

          I suspect no chaos: I am convinced of
          the cosmos in your company, Walt Whitman!
          I greet you, sir, as America's great voice.

Well, you've come to be disillusioned, have you ?

          Disillusioned? Not after Colorado!
          Red rocks are a foolish place in which to look
          for inspiration, but a fine one to forget
          you ever had any. Disillusioned, here?
          There is no one in this wide America
          of yours whom I love and honour half so much:
          I came to see you without the illusion
          of a ground-glass lens between us, Walt Whitman!

Look your fill, look close enough
and you may even
see my beard growing : I fear I have
been photographed until the cameras themselves
are tired of me. The real man
by now is a poor
replacement—you and a good proofreader
must puzzle me out : I don't feel worth my weight
in feathers, not even quills.

Not pinions but pens! It must be so, for
every prophet, I discover, reads his proofs.
Do I disturb you when you are not yourself?
Your health is not all it might have been today?

My health is hell,
and heaven is the first moment after
constipation. There is no purgatory . . .
Here, come round, no this way—stand
where I can see you.
Dr. Bucke gave me no clue . . .

. . . A doctor is all very well when you *are,*
but only then—then they can offer comfort!
When one is ill, doctors are most depressing.

Bucke's
not that breed : he tends the mad, in Canada—
a kind of medical mystic,
he lets me call him,
and his letter gave no hint you were
such a great boy ! I feared a man wizened
by the frost of worldliness,
but for all that fur—
it *is* fur, isn't it ? Not a mane ?

You *are the lion, sir, between the two of us.*

Well, you're no lamb, judging by the look of you.
From the set of your shoulders,
one would say you had
the American I AM in you somewhere . . .

15

In Boston they took me up, or on, for Irish;
in Baltimore, for British—in each city
they seem ready to take me for what I am.
But I am not a boy, sir. Is it my fault
if I seem young because I look behind me,
and you as old as you do because you look
so far ahead? Future of mind, you have that,
where presence is the most one hopes for. I saw
a man in the West whose twig bends near water—
I call on you as one consults such a man.

You know how to say
    the remembered, if not the right thing.
If I can't speak poetry, I can inspire it—
        I swim in your flattery, son.

Better swim than drown, in any element.
Never heed our ages, Walt (may I call you
Walt? I must be Oscar to you). We meet here
as prophets: at ease in Zion, without age,
without agitation, and I hope to find
you feeling the better for that.

I am as you see:
    incarcerated in this one chair.
What is prophetic about that?

                            What we share.
        The gift of prophecy is given to all
        who do not know what will happen to themselves.

        You may be Ezra—
    I know; day by day I learn:
the trouble with me
    is not what I do but what I don't
feel. My fingers are dead . . .

O put them in mine, Walt. Doctors prate of chills,
but I think any man who has survived your
American newspapers is impregnable.
And your décor! I have been dashing between
coyotes and cañons, only to discover
one is a ravine and the other a fox—
I don't know which, I believe they change about.

So it would have been
with me, a like confusion
if I had ventured
abroad : foreign landscape, foreign livestock!
I am homesick enough right here in Camden.
America is the one
country you can be
homesick for while you are in it—one
big case of homesickness. I would have frozen
solid if I had taken
Tennyson's offer.

You would have discovered that Lord Tennyson
believes himself constituted to protest
against all modern improvements: he regards
(I think I should warn you, Walt) America
as a modern improvement—one of the worst!

You give the literary man a touch
of frostbite over there, and he is never
quite the man he was, after
London has set in.
I do not regret never getting
myself to England : how would England have helped
or hurt the *Leaves*, for instance?

The leaves—ah, Leaves of Grass! *I have always thought*
spears *your word, my dear Walt*—Spears of Grass: *you are*
a naked man, you know, bearing a naked spear . . .

Leaves is what I wrote
and what I wear, if my nakedness
must be covered. Spears? I want no defences.
All this fear of indecency,
all this noise about
purity and the social order
is nasty—too nasty to compromise with.
I never come up against it
but I think of what
Heine said to a lady who had
expressed some suspicions about the body :
"Madame," Heine said to her,

''are not all of us
    naked under our clothes?'' I say so,
I got it all said in the *Leaves*, Oscar. Sex
            is the word when you mean sex,
discredited here
    with us, rejected from art, but still
the root of our life, the life below the life.

       You are with the prophets, Walt, when you speak so.
       I can imagine Isaiah, hearing you . . .
       In Idaho, Isaiah would have been as
       you appear: Isaiah in a red cravat.

       Spare me Isaiah, spare me
the responsibility.
    The *Leaves* is a this-side book, Oscar.
And as for landscape, all we need is grit,
       the body's grit, not to fall,
as Emerson fell,
    short of earth: after the shadow, not
the fact. Grit is the guarantee of the rest—
       coyotes here, castles there.

       A this-side book? Some love it on that side, Walt;
       some worship. In the scriptures of modern Europe
       I can cite no verses—though I've brought you mine,
       bound to order in grass-green (I have noticed
       the public is largely influenced by the look
       of a book. So are we all. It is the one
       artistic thing about the public) . . . These are
       First Poems, an offering honored to be held
       between your hands—warmer now, are they not?
       I was saying, Walt, before vanity came
       between us (though I do not wish to appear
       to run vanity down), I was saying that
       I can conceive of no Bible worthy, save
       yours and Baudelaire's, to prepare mankind
       for an identical body and soul. Leaves
       of Grass, Flowers of Evil: *our sacred botany!*

Is that meant to be
    a joke, Oscar—flowers of evil?

What grows out of the ground ... It is a mystery,
                    and had better remain so.
I am glad to have
        your book : don't apologize for First
Poems. Books are like men, the best of them have flaws.
                Thank God for the flaws—if not
for the flaws, Oscar,
        love would be impossible.

> *I think it is, Walt, flaws and all, unless*
> *you link the temperament of a vampire*
> *to the discretion of an anemone ...*

            Is that
the evil flower you speak of—anemones ?
                Even sea-anemones ?

> Les Fleurs du Mal—*poems by Charles Baudelaire,*
> *Walt: the greatest moralist to sing in France*
> *since Villon was imprisoned.*

Do moralists sing ?
        I thought they expurgated poems.
French or Hebrew, it is all one to me :
                prophets, moralists, bibles
make me uneasy.
        I want picnics and the freedom to loaf,
a jolly all-round good time, with the parsons
                and police uninvited.
I have always been
        a first-rate aquatic loafer, could
float on my back forever ... Indecency
                is always invoked against
floating and growing.
        What kind of a gardener is your
Baudelaire ? Are his flowers indecent, like mine ?
                Were some plucked up by the roots ?

> *The book was censored, the poems were called obscene*
> *when they appeared—a short while after yours, Walt.*
> *Their interest is not that they were suppressed*
> *by a foolish official, but that they were*
> *written by a great artist.*

19

"Foolish officials"
     can be interesting too, Oscar,
I found that out. Secretary Harlan took
        the *Leaves* so seriously
he abstracted them
     —the proof sheets, it was, not the book yet—
from my desk drawer, at night, after I had gone,
        put them back again, neat, and
next day discharged me!
     It will not do to fly in the face
of courts and conformity; it did not do
        at all well for me, Oscar.

> *I shall cross that bridge*
> *after I have burned it behind me. I know*
> *it is not my past people so much object to—*
> *I do not yet have a past—but my future . . .*

And they objected
     to Baudelaire? What was it he wrote,
Oscar, can you say it out? I never could
        say mine . . . I never commit
poems to memory:
     they would be in my way.

> *If I cannot hear Walt Whitman's Calamus*
> *from his lips, I am happy to be the first*
> *to bring Baudelaire's artistry to his ears.*

     I have heard
a good deal with these ears, son. I find it hard
        to imagine a shock
in that direction.
     Even the *Leaves* are no longer said
to be lewd: nothing is harder to keep up
        than a bad reputation.
Try a flower
     on me, Oscar, try me with a bloom
from the wicked bed. Speak it in English, though—
        I can neither hear nor read
a Frenchman's language.
     Speak your piece, Oscar, I am all ears
to meet my fellow-evangelist . . .

And I all eagerness, Walt. Not until
you permit a poet a mask does he dare
tell the truth ...

I dared.
Do not suppose that the *Leaves*
is a mask. It is the man,
the life a man can live in language.
He must tell it himself—no disciple can.

Is it not incredible, then,
that the prospect of having a biographer
has tempted no one to renounce having
a life?

There can be no renouncing,
you have to get on
with it. Do get on with it, Oscar.

My memory will serve to recite
but not to recreate the music: I translate
line by line, trusting the mystery. It is
an early piece, no less perfect than the late:
only mediocrites progress—masters
revolve.

I was never quite so certain of myself,
Oscar, that I could afford
to revolve. To write
on and on, to the end, even if
in senility ... To make a complete record—
there's more to say, always more ...
Now let me hear it,
this crudity of your Baudelaire.

It is a poem entitled "Spleen."

"Spleen"? In the way of resentment? anger?
Well, we are not forever
patted on the back—
sometimes we are kicked in the behind ...
"Spleen," then. Say on.

"I am even as the king of a rainy country,
Rich but impotent, senile though still young,
Who wearies of his courtiers' flattery
Nor hunts with hawk or hound, nor heeds the while
His subjects starve outside the palace walls.
His favorite fool no longer brings a smile
To cruel eyes incredulous of doom.
The royal bed becomes a royal tomb,
And ladies who might find all princes fair
Game, no longer gaud themselves enough
To win a glance from this cold skeleton.
His alchemist turns lead to gold, yet fails
To draw the dark corruption from his soul,
And even bloodbaths in true Roman style
(Such as old warriors regard with shame)
Cannot relume a living corpse whose veins
No blood but Lethe's livid absinthe stains."

"... king of a rainy country ..."
I know what that means, Oscar:
I live by the sound
        of rain, imaginary rainfall.
And I am used to defections—how often
                young enthusiasts grow old,
yes, old and cold too.
        Still, if the world is unjust to you,
you must take care not to be unjust to the world.
                I don't get much beyond that
with "Spleen": what I hear
        is a sickly sensuality in it,
the sensuality of convalescence—
                you might call it that, you might ...
I don't care. It's all
        too bad to be true. "Livid absence"?

No, absinthe, *Walt, a liquor brewed from wormwood.*

I know absinthe—in New Orleans a man drank it,
                or said he did. I saw him
dip his fingers in,
        wet his eyebrows, eyelids, faint dead away.
So his "Lethe" is real ...

It is a way of getting rid of the real.

Bad riddance! It sounds
as if the man could pity
himself alone, not
seriously pity other men.
Is it not verse written of malice prepense,
all laid out, rhymed, designed on
mathematical
principles—is it not a machine,
a kind of enslavement?

Yes, it is Art, it bears the fetters of Art.
Ah, Walt, and you make no slaves—only lovers.
I shall not be so foolish as to defend
one genius from another. Disaffection
is inseparable from faith: I often
betray myself with a kiss. Surprising, though,
you are not more taken by the Criminal . . .

. . . the Morbid, you mean?
I am not taken by that.

Americans I have met are certainly
great hero-worshippers, and always
adopt their heroes from the criminal classes . . .

The *Leaves* is a book
written for the criminal classes.

How on earth do you come to such a notion?

I don't come to it—it's the case; the others
have no need for a poet.

Are you in the criminal classes yourself?

Certainly, why not?

I was hoping you might get me in as well.
Only the utterly worthless can be reformed—
I feel beyond reform—I want only Form.
Is it not Form, Walt, that keeps things together?

I keep nothing together.
Look around : have I
ever kept anything together?
Body and soul, that's all I keep together.

You keep them splendidly. That simplicity
has been the great enclosing secret for you.
All the same, along the way, I should suppose
there were distinctions, even in criminal
classes . . . Our failure is, we form habits . . .
In Idaho, Walt, they took me to visit
their prison—apparently a model one.
There was all the odd prey of humanity
in hideous striped suits, making bricks in the sun.
I saw one man, a murderer with steel eyes,
spending the interval before he was hanged
in reading novels—a poor apprenticeship,
I thought, for facing either God or Nothing . . .

It was for just such a man
I wrote *Leaves of Grass:*
a man reading in a jail, as well
as any other man who cares to read me.
. . . No one was ever bad enough
to be put in jail;
he was, or might be, bad enough to be
put in a hospital. But all this judging
is not a habit—more likely
it is a disease.
I don't hold with judging, measuring,
weighing this offence against that penalty.
Breaking loose is the only thing,
opening new ways.
But once a man breaks loose, or starts to,
or even thinks he'll start, he should be sure he knows
what he has undertaken.
I expected hell.
I got it. Nothing that has occurred
came as a surprise : probably more's to come.
That won't surprise me either.

To me, Walt, it must come as a surprise—life
is so often nothing more than a quotation.

Most people are other people. Surprises
change life: I have more, I am sure, than I deserve,
but it is always nice to have a little more
than one deserves . . .

There is no ''deserves,''
      Oscar. I never weighed what I gave
for what I got, but I'm glad of what I got.
              What did I get—do you know?
Well, I got the boys,
      for one thing: the boys, hundreds of them.
They were, they are, they will be mine. I gave myself
           for them: myself. And I got
the boys. Then I got
      the *Leaves*, not spears but *Leaves of Grass.*
Without the boys—if it had not been for the boys,
          I never would have had the *Leaves,*
the consummated
      book, the last confirming word.   —Oscar! . . .
What are you doing down there? Have you lost
          your seat or your senses?

                    Walt, you've gained another boy.
      It will not give you another poem for
      the Leaves, *but I want to ask something of you.*
      A favor, Walt . . .

I reckoned there must be a reason for you
          to visit another kind
of model prison.
      More than to give me your book, and more
than to get me down to Baudelaire's level.
          I think I know the reason,
I usually can guess
      why a man comes to see me. You want
more than a handshake with Walt Whitman, you want
          to know what you must give up!
You see me here, alone
      in this chair, at this window, you take
my hands to ward off the chill, and you wonder
          how to go about giving
yourself away . . .

Walt, you must bless me, I want
to take your blessing with me. I cannot leave
you my book, it is not the book I must write
for Walt Whitman—that poem will come, bless me
and it will *come, from a deeper place than these . . .*
Let me have my book again.

What, Indian-giving? Do you know
the sense of that, boy? Taking back what you give!

I have nothing to give you—yet. Here, for now,
Walt, my buttonhole—the tribute of a flower . . .

Not an evil one, I trust!
Even on your knees,
Oscar, not a flower of evil . . .

One harmless heliotrope, Walt, for your
hand on my forehead . . .

I dressed many a wound, Oscar, with this hand
which can feel nothing now:
but the boys I nursed
had suffered their fate: yours is yet to come.
Take my blessing with your book, boy. They're both yours.

You have instructed me
past hopes—past fears. In you, Walt, I discover
how a desire becomes a destiny. To give
myself away! Not to make sacrifices
but to be *one. To be, somehow, holy, like you—*
Walt, what else does sacrifice mean?

I am a sick old man on Mickle Street, boy,
I am not a holy man;
or *all* men are. Then
you understand me? Or maybe I
understand you now. To me, you see, the *Leaves*
is an essential poem—
it needed making,
like an essential life needs living.
Maybe yours will be an essential life—
one needing to have been lived!

Give me the best man
over the best books—books are not facts,
merely the effort to master facts. I say
effort because I'm not sure
of much else . . .

> . . . *Life, Walt, you make me **sure***
> *of life! Your hand—I am truly your boy* . . .

Kiss me,
and catch your trolly, I've lectured long
enough. You must read the writing on the wall,
or the page, or on the face,
by yourself, Oscar.
You must find it, you can't be told it . . .
My own preference is for texts that can be
carried in the pocket.

> *Walt . . . You have scored a triumph for America.*
> *I came, I saw, I was conquered! Not by fame,*
> *though anything is better than virtuous*
> *obscurity—not fame conquered, but life,*
> *your life, your immortality!*

Not
immortality,
Oscar, identity : call it that
and we are one.

> You've *won,*
> *Walt. I am with you, and so I leave you,*
> *with gratitude and honor and all my love.*
> *Good-bye* . . .

Good-bye, son. Mary Davis!
Show Mr. Wilde how to go—
the trolly is at
the end of Mickle Street . . . Give him one
of our umbrellas if it's raining still.
. . . Thank you, Mary, that's enough.
No, I don't want you
fussing, I want to empty this room.

I can still see him, in front of the window,
                    a dim reflection of Oscar,
talking about art.
          I can still hear him, as if he's there.
The North his needle points to is only art.
                    Art is always only art.
But a great boy, still,
          a great manly boy. While he was here
I think I found the haystack in his needle . . .
                    Did you notice if he left
a green book downstairs,
          on the table by the door? Nothing
there? Well, that's the right thing. Put this in water—
                    this "harmless heliotrope,"
leave it by the bed . . .
          There are some things too big for the world—
they crowd it out at the sides. They need more room
                    than Camden can supply them,
or Canada either—
          Look at that color! Can anyone
state the whole case for the universe? I need
                    a nap, Mary, get me back
into bed, I want
          time to myself, now.

A PHENOMENON
OF NATURE

for Nancy Marchand

1898

'How long, O Capriped?' How long, Sophie—
it is no joke—must we clamber on?
Is there no end to this cliff-hanging?
You have had your revenge, or I am
having it, step by step—now no more
steps, merely to prove you were surprised.

Surprised? Of course, but what is not surprising?
I am forever being
surprised: that the sun troubles to reappear,
that I do not dissolve in the bath ... It is
possibly a talent, no?

It is a tolerance, Sophie, for
that tempting range of relevancies
known to us as the universe. Your
talent is masked by your temperament:
you are a good woman, in the worst
sense of the word. And a tireless one!
I cannot climb forever upward—
sit down for a moment. Where are you
taking me, just because I took you
aback—were you taken all that far?

All that. All that I have a 'tolerance' for.
Fortunately there were no feathers on hand,
or I should have been knocked down and never got
up again. No one warned me
when the bell rang for zweite Frühestück *and I*
stepped into the reading-room—

though why the Quisisana calls it that
I cannot think: no one ever reads *in there,*
> *or anywhere on Capri!*
Dear Master, they have no literature here,
merely the memoranda for mimicry.

> In the minds of Italians, my dear
> —they do have minds: I have seen Duse—
> it is better to marry than to learn.

We learned, if we learned, by marrying others,
leaving ourselves to burn . . . out. Ashes now. No—
> *I will not speak of our past,*
I promised myself if I saw you again . . .

> Our past, Sophie—*ours?* The case we
> fasten to crucial experience
> is dominantly genitive—my
> defeat, your rival, her death . . . Our past.
> We possess whatever possesses
> us, as we discover when we breathe . . .

Or whatever we have failed to possess . . . as
> *we discover when we choke.*
When I found I was not alone (as I am,
for the most part) I suffered a moment's qualm—
> *I confess I was startled . . .*

> My being in the same room with you
> does not mean less of a solitude,
> Sophie—it may mean more of a prison.

I have been free, and alone, some twenty years:
I am old enough, now, to take my chances—
in the open air, above the opening sea.

> Must you take mine as well, on these rocks?
> I fear you have lost them already,
> writing as you did, writing at all!

Master, I am in my high middle ages!
To you, women are tragic, women stand for

the tragic course, the curse of nature itself;
  but I have learned otherwise—
I have learned other woes than the tragic kind.
Ah, we are comic, after a certain point:
whatever is natural is so unfair!
Our breasts become apparitions, our navel
  almost an operation . . .
One morning I looked at the glass suddenly,
and I laughed—the way one laughs at Goldoni—
and broke the silence which was the thing we had
  instead of a tradition.

> The thing we had instead of having . . .
> Traditions that have lost their meaning
> are the hardest to destroy . . . You wrote—

What could I write that did not go without saying?
  So of course I said it, wrote
in ignorance of what may come of writing . . .
You cannot conceive how strange that moment was:
  before my eyes stood a man
all in black, turning over old newspapers—
so fierce, so foreign, so formidable, I thought:
if he were twenty years younger, that could be
  the Master . . . *And so it was.*
You had my letters, you heard my call: you came!
No answer all that time—you were the answer,
you were your own last word. My qualm was quelled then,
  I was not seeing a ghost,
I was merely aghast at my own . . . success.

> Nothing is my last word, Sophie, not
> even myself; myself least of all.
> There are always extenuations,
> always stages in self-forgiveness . . .
> Wherefore your 'success,' my dear. I had—
> I lived, let us say, so my enemies
> might define themselves. I have *out*lived
> the best of that lot—reality means
> elimination, as I tried to show them—
> in the battles of drama there are
> no victors, only survivors. Now,
> without enemies, I have had to fall

31

back on my friends! That is only my
little joke, my dear: when our vices
have grown so great we can no longer
hide them, we begin to boast of them—
ultimately we begin to boast
even of that, as I am doing.
You see me because ... I am no ghost,
Sophie, as you guessed in the hotel:
Ghosts do not stumble uphill or gasp
for breath, ghosts do not long for brandy—
ghosts you may have only if you let
none of them return altogether.

Let *them return! Surely it is a wiser course*
to invite them ... Oh, I know what you believe
about Ghosts. And *returning.*
The problem is not that I cannot escape
my ghosts—the problem is that I have escaped
my ghosts so successfully.
My limitations have always been the earth—
the earth and the present, here and now. Master,
what if the past is an illusion of language?
What if the past does not exist?

It is all that exists—which is why
it is invisible to you, Sophie.
There is an illusion, you are right—
we are united in social life—
and what else is language if not
the life we lead together (no, don't
interrupt, you merely prove my point)
—we are united by an illusion,
by a tacit claim that there has been
no past. But there is that other life
we call our own, the life by whose light
or whose darkness, more likely darkness,
participation in the past is not
a duty. It is necessity.

I do not recognize it!
Necessity is only what has happened:
it did not have to be that way.

No, my dear, but so we chose it. Not
the blind inevitability
we always ascribe to what we did,
to what was done. You misunderstand:
it is only the present which is
inevitable. The past—even 'ours'—
could have been otherwise, but not now;
there are no accidents now, nothing
but the furies mad in pursuit. Ghosts!
Well, my dear, you at least read—even here,
out on these terrible rocks you read.
And I know you write: letters—letters ...
Receiving letters unfits one for
any reply. The reading spirit
shuts the book of wounds. Sophie, I came
to Capri, not to you. My purpose—

I know, I know! That purpose of yours, Master—
half Europe knows: to conclude your 'Epilogue,'
the new play. Why else would I ...

A foregone conclusion, I fear. New?
It is the last play. And the last work;
I mean it to be—only the whole
can invent a detail. I am old now,
and I need ... what old men need. Sophie,
in letter after letter you said ...

I said nothing—but I promised what you had,
all you had before. Do you remember that?
Do you remember what the island has? Look
at those gulls, they are below
us, almost underfoot, yet how high they soar:
we are nearly where we were—
I sat right here to write those letters of mine,
above the secret spaces of the sea ... Oh,
I have no secrets from you!
Are there indeed such things, I wonder, as secrets?

Indeed there are. Everyone knows them.
I knew mine early. And I have lived
according to them—to one secret—
a life formed, if not broken, by stern

process, inexorable persistence.
I knew early that it was my task
to attain the clarity of . . . what?
Consequences, say, and then to die,
once the consequence was disclosed . . .
Assiduously I searched out, and found,
my direction, pursued it with that
'merciless' memory of mine, right
to the end. Sophie, this is the end.
Without memory we could not die!
Where could 'imagination' come from,
if not from memory? No secrets . . .
I knew always that my task would be
to say what we lack and what we have:
that is our unity. To say that,
then silence. You cannot promise me
what I had before—only what comes
of what I had. I do not want the past,
although I cannot help having it.
I need the present. I came for that.

And found no more than me, is it not so? left
over, yet ever present.
Can you not have, here, better and different
presences: sun, sea, light, shade—opportunities,
pleasures—than you had in Christiania?
Why rust there, sitting in a corner like Zola,
observing the same cobwebs
and thinking of obscene occurrences? Why
wipe the blade of your mind there, as though after
a meal where bones were severed?
Well, you've come! and I swear not to bother you,
not even to speak to you!

Oh for God's sake, Sophie, speak, speak . . .
You cannot 'bother' me. I am no
companion for myself. I must not
be alone with myself—that is why
I write: to write is to say *I am*
not the only one. But even here
above the blue surge and the white surf,
I am the Babylon I must go
out of, or I perish . . . Do you know

why I let you lure me back to this—
this *nature* you celebrate so much,
this wrack and ruin of rock and sea?
Do you know why I am ready, now,
for what was ruin to become model?
Because nature is *already there.*
Because I do not have to make it.
'To Capri then I came'... an old man
exhausted by his own energies.

Not old, Master, you must not keep saying 'old'
        and then squander energy
in every phrase, as it were bits and pieces
of aphorism and epigram and even oracle...
        There is no such thing as 'old,'
we are always in the middle: middle age
        is living until the last,
and then it is still the heart of life, it is
still life 'in the midst of death,' no? Exhausted—
twenty years ago you were exhausted, too,
but they were never yours, never ours, those
        energies: they are of earth,
the energies that bear us on. Get up now,
Master, we have no more than a little way ...

            'Master'—I am not the master here!

Up, I say, and come with me—

                Those energies have borne me *down:* work
                has weighed me to the earth. One after
                the next, each play is a huge graveyard—
                on most of the slabs the names have worn
                down—a dramatist buries his dead
                in the one grave. Even here I am
                burdened—in Norway I have no rest ...
                I begin to see: the triumphant
                experience of genius is sleep.
                What I could do was not to be done:
                what I have done is to be undone.

You speak as if you were ill, or had been ill.

In twenty years you have not once been ill—nor
before that; your wife told me . . .

A man's wife knows too much about him.
I have never been really ill; perhaps
for that reason I have never been
really well. Capri will cure my . . . health?

Master, let me show you what is here, nature
on the island that you can
take upon you, for yourself. Fifty steps more
and we stand where Tiberius ruled the world . . .

One only took our nature upon Him.
I will not take this one upon me,
here where an emperor heard the cry—
'Great Pan is dead!' No religion here,
it is hopeless, like literature
on Capri—it is hopeless for me:
I am the blank page betwen the Old
and the New Testament, I cannot—

You need not, Master: you said you did not have
to invent it: only look around you! Here
nature is a god, surely.

No, only evidence there are gods,
greater than Roman emperors! Need—
there is only one need: I told you
the word—it is what comes with sleep: dreams.
Tiberius, Julian—the fate of the world
entrusted to former children—sick
children who acclaimed themselves gods.
For a child or a sick man, nothing
is harder than to tell what he dreams
truthfully. Only the clearest mind
can lay down the landmarks of sleep.
Write over every nursery door,
Sophie, in purple ink: This Too Will
Pass. And we see what it passes *to*.

To this. Look there! Have you ever seen the like?
A place where nothing passes,

nothing is at an end, so nothing stands still.
There is the sea, down there, straight down, below us,
*   breathing its cautious insomnia,*
driven here, there, with only itself to love,
and the sun above us, giving our bodies
*   away to themselves, to us:*
it will be reason enough for coming here, for
being, if you read the sea beneath you, take
*   that experience of life . . .*

> I need no experience of life.
> Any travelling salesman, Sophie,
> has seen more of life than I. Playwrights
> are too busy writing plays to see
> life—my occupation is to dig
> some filler out of *Dagbladet*
> and brood upon the foolishness until
> it falls like tea-leaves into fate—
> not to waste time experiencing!
> Beyond a certain age there is one
> problem only—the problem of time.

But the Mediterranean, Master!
the sea, the sun, this timeless brilliant air . . .

> All art need not be sunstruck, Sophie,
> nor every writer jump onto the *train bleu.*
> You want to show me how our shadows
> are cast before us, down the cliff face . . .

Yes, Master: here we are like coming events.

> Or departing ones. Tiberius . . .

Come to the brink, Master, and see how the waves
make for themselves a salvation by giving
*   way to the rocks down there, oh*
graceful to the point of dentistry—just look—
*   Mein Gott! What is it, Master?*
What has happened? Why are you hugging that root?
*   Did you fall? Are you all right?*

> . . . Never sick, Susanna told you? What
> did she know? What do you? I have a fear . . .

Did you bring me here to murder me?
On heights I find myself prone to ...
I find myself prone—as you find me:
Sophie, I have escaped with my life
from the clutch of a giant hand! BACK—
get me back from here before I fall ...

There is no danger, Master, no accident
is possible: did you not say so yourself?
No harm can come to us here. Your gaze will give
        life to what is locked within
its ring—Master, you are king of the mountain!

I cannot run the risk—I cannot run,
Sophie, I cannot leave the spot. No—
my work is not yet done, I cannot
fail now, fall here, because the earth
may just this once subside ... I have found
that what we fear, we make happen.

Or make human. Master, you cannot fail or fall:
the earth will hold you—if you hold it fast.
        Do as I say, surrender
to the earth—where else would you find your play?
In the earth there is no time, Master—no past.
        Press your body to the soil,
dig your fingers in the ground, become the earth,
        receive yourself—like the sea ...
Twenty years I have followed you, Master, followed
        as each play came from the next,
the inevitable future growing day by day
        into the irrevocable present.
Now you follow me, you be my audience—
Master, lie down again, here, put your head in my lap,
take a fresh cigar. You will get over this ...

No, I may get used to it. No one
gets over things. It is things we get
under, and when they are on top of us
then we are used to them. I have come
back from the earth, alive, only to find ...
I have never lived. A dead man. All

the others, every clerk and copyist . . .
I have never lived—never, never.

No one has. We only do.
What is it now, Master—why do you stare so?

Because I see it. So that is why
I came here! Thank you, Sophie, thank you
for giving me this last . . . as once you . . .

I gave you Hilda Wangel?
Did I—was she me? Tell me, please, Master, please!

. . . I see it, yes: a man following
a woman over the rocks . . . to death.
I shall do it my own way, not yours.

Doing things your own way—is that doing them?

Well, having them your own way is not
having them. A sick emperor, Sophie,
a second childhood here in your arms . . .

Master, this is the safe earth.

Safe! You are on fire!—here, I have burnt
your dress—my cigar—throw it away!
The sea will serve for something—put it out!

Sign the hole, Henrik—sign it and I shall be
a rich woman. Indeed, with you here, lying
in my arms, resting, saving . . .
I shall have an embarrassment of riches.

Riches, Sophie, are *meant* to compose
an embarrassment. I am ready
to go back down. Down to work, now
the work is waiting. Give me your arm.
Easier to descend than to climb . . .
Half the people we know or will know
are dead at any given moment—
and this is a given moment, Sophie,
you have given it to me—yet
how many corpses have we seen?
Slowly now, my dear: we shall be safe.

THE LESSON OF
THE MASTER

for Sanford Friedman

... Edith Wharton was here, an angel of devastation in her
wondrous, cushioned, *general* car.   HENRY JAMES

Paris—Versailles, 1912

No,
>   not out the window.
There is a receptacle under the seat:
if the tray is full, please empty the ashes
>   there, Mr. Roseman.

>   *And if the receptacle is full,*
>   *I suppose we could open the door.*
>   *After all, Mrs. Wharton, they're not* his.

>   Indeed they are not!
His I hold here, and shall not let them leave me:
they will not go until the urn itself
>   turns to earth again.
Ping!
>   don't snap at our guest,
he's only doing as I ask. Lie down, Pong,
lie down! Orderliness about *my* ashes
is an action, Mr. Roseman, not a passion,
>   as you might suppose:
I have not replaced the carriage-and-pair
with a Delage merely to litter the road
>   with my own leavings.
Need the Bois de Boulogne be ashen behind
my poor little cortège, as well as before?

> *Not until Ville d'Avray. Rain and mud*
> *it "needs" to be, in order to be*
> *reality, orderly or not.*
> *Once we get to Ville d'Avray, Corot*
> *has the last word—he is the last word*
> *in ashes, don't you think, Mrs. Wharton?*
> *All that gray and silver, all that blur!*
> *Until then, of course, the ashes are*
> *yours—so many, or so much (what does*
> *one say in the case of ashes? much*
> *or many? A writer ought to know . . .)*

My cigarettes leave
many ashes. The ashes of a man are
much . . . too much to bear alone. Too much for me.
That is why I asked for company, Mr. Roseman:
    I need another
presence here, now, if I am to reach Versailles
in countenance to face the cemetery;
till then I do not want to be quite alone.
    I want you to help . . .

> *. . . To help bear the ashes? They are yours*
> *as well. All that he left, the leavings . . .*
> *Provided I can fill a function,*
> *I am pleased to help you—emptying*
> *is a function like any other,*
> *except filling, of course. And I can*
> *empty as fast as you can fill—almost.*
> *How much you smoked that other time, or*
> *at least how many, snapping up one*
> *gold-tipped Egyptian after the next!*
> *Even then you would not wait to grow*
> *an ash before you ground out the glow.*
> *In fact, when I first met you, I thought . . .*

Met me—you met me?

> *. . . At Howard Overing's, in London.*
> *Isn't that why you asked me to come?*

No, I asked Mr. James particularly
to suggest someone I had not met, someone
    whom I did not know.

On such a journey—this is not the first time
I have escorted to a cemetery
    what are called remains,
though it will be the last, as long as I remain—
the last remainder, as Mr. Scribner says . . .
    Someone whom I know!
On such a journey one may say anything,
and prefers, of course, to say it to no one
    in particular.

> *I am no one in particular,*
> *Mrs. Wharton, you don't know me; I*
> *know you. I know you in general.*

You know my novels,
you mean: you have read me? That is not the same . . .
One reads most writers to escape knowing them.

> *No, I mean I spent an afternoon—*
> *last year—with you in London. Of course*
> *you don't remember me distinctly,*
> *individually. How could you?*
> *I was one of the shadows, a mere*
> *hypothesis of furniture: the one*
> *Overing introduced as "a friend*
> *of Gerald's"—and we were all his friends,*
> *you, and Mr. James, and the rest of us,*
> *the shadows . . . Who could remember that?*

I hope Gerald could . . .
Over the gate of Hell must be written HERE
EVERYTHING IS REMEMBERED. I am in
    no more than Limbo
since Gerald died. Forgive me, Mr. Roseman,
I do not mean to be rude, but since we did
meet, as you say, why on earth should Mr. James
suggest you be a party to my sad errand . . . ?

> *I haven't the faintest idea.*
> *Perhaps because on earth an errand*
> *means a mistake as well, Mrs. Wharton.*
> *I don't pretend to know Mr. James's*
> *reason—he has so many. Or so much?*

Well, he *meets* so many. He meets more and more
people : reason enough to make more and more
mistakes—in order to be more and more alone,
I sometimes think. Gerald used to say he had
been spared only—

> *—to be by-passed. Gerald was not spared.*

How did you know that—
how do you know what Gerald said of Mr. James?

> *Mrs. Wharton, though you may not recall*
> *meeting me, I was presented to you*
> *as Gerald's friend. Men speak to their friends,*
> *and Gerald spoke to me. Even of you*
> *he would speak . . .*

He would speak of me?
To you? Gerald discussed me with his . . . his friends?

> *As you know, he rarely*
> *let his good things go unrepeated.*

They bore repeating.

> *Were you bored? I never was, Mrs. Wharton.*

Nor I, Mr. Roseman.
If you must, then, they are *worth* repeating, those
    ''good things'' of Gerald's.
As I suppose what he said of me to be :
    worth repeating : now.

> *Surely. He called you "the self-made man"—*
> *it became the phrase for you among*
> *his friends. Don't you find it becoming?*
> *"Edith Wharton is a self-made man . . ."*

Inevitably
the case, I'm sure you can see, when one starts life
as a woman. To men of my father's world,
    which was Gerald's world—
my great-grandfather married a Mackenzie—

to men of that world, who made it a bold choice
to have *books* in the room called the library,
     women were a toast,
or they were nothing: a woman never went
out if she expected men to come to her.
Authorship was regarded—though *regarded*
is scarcely the word—as something between
a black art and a form of manual labor:
     either enterprise,
for a lady, equally unsuitable.
That is why I owe so much—owe everything
to Gerald. He found me when my mind was starved,
and he fed me till our last hour together.

> *Yes, Gerald was a great feeder for*
> *late hours. Spanish hours, you might call them,*
> *they were that late. When we were in Spain,*
> *he used to say ... Well, you know what he said.*
> *And it helped you—it fed you, fed your mind?*
> *So you were not, entirely, self-made.*

     Entirely selfish,
you mean? Perhaps—perhaps not. I never had
your opportunities in Spain to find out.
We saw each other here, Rue de Varenne,
     and when the end came
I promised him the grave in Versailles. With mine,
     when it is my time.

> *I have never seen the American*
> *graveyard in Versailles, but I suppose*
> *the associations would please him:*
> *how far-sighted you've been, Mrs. Wharton.*

One sees beyond the senses. I hesitate
to imagine what the life of the spirit
     would have been to me
without Gerald Mackenzie. Had it not been
for him, I should have turned out to be
no more than another of those lectured-to
ladies who mean to have the best culture, quite
     as they mean to have
the best plumbing; they like to let culture run

over them as the hot water does, you know,
    without much effort.

> *And you made an effort. Much effort,*
> *in fact. Certainly you did not leave*
> *Mr. Wharton because he lectured you—*
> *you were a lady who turned out*
> *otherwise: you turned out many books.*

I turned into them, if you must have the phrase.
    They were an effort
my husband could not endure, even before
his illness—before we had to live apart.
No distractions: he was quite given over
to the New York of families and fortunes.
A trivial society gains significance
    from the life it gags.
Money-making in New York is so strenuous
that men and women never meet socially
    before dinner-hours.
If I was a failure in Boston because
I was thought too fashionable to be serious,
    in New York I failed
because I was feared to be too serious
    to be fashionable.

> *But you did not fail—you left. If that's*
> *failing, then Gerald failed, and Mr. James,*
> *and even I—then all of us failed!*
> *And certainly Gerald never failed—*
> *he pulled up his stakes for higher ones:*
> *that was one of his "good things," wasn't it?*
> *Something of the kind. If leaving is*
> *failing, then which of us failed—to leave?*

Not Teddy—Mr. Wharton. He was a success, there.
Too much of one ever to leave his New York,
though Gerald called him "Teddy Bore" for it—did he
    repeat that one too?
Wonderful to bores and children, Teddy was;
you really should have seen the man with children!
Now to me the devil frequently appeared

45

in the shape of a child, but he could never
deceive me as to his true identity—
I was always aware of it, and eschewed
    all contact with him
under that disguise . . . Teddy could not endure
my disbelief in children. Nor could Gerald
endure Teddy. When I had to make a choice,
I chose my books and Gerald—I chose my books
    because of Gerald.
I chose to make something of myself : a divorce
is a great creator, as I was to learn.

       "Marriage, divorce and death make barren
       our lives." Swinburne—wrong, as usual:
       you had all three from Teddy Wharton, and
       lived to tell . . . many tales. You made up
       a new kind of life for yourself, then?

    I was left alone
with time : I became what is called an author.
Not a poet, like Swinburne. Poets write something,
authors write about something. My dear young man,
whatever we manage to do is merely
    a modification
of what we have failed to do. So when we fail,
it is only because we have given up.

       But you have given up nothing! All
       you had is within reach, Mrs. Wharton—
       like Ping and Pong, like the ashtray there . . .

    . . . and the ashes here.

       Exactly. You must have read my mind.

I read what is legible. Little enough.
    Until now, you see,
Gerald was not within reach. To me he was
a man who could take nothing from another,
but gave, gave only, as he would give to me,
    and gave to the end.

46

What was it you wanted him to take?

What I had : myself. By the time I had made
something to give him worth the taking : nothing.
    Freedom is nothing,
it was nothing to Gerald, only to me.
But if you have made something, you need someone
to offer it to—the freedom you have made
    by making up lives,
even if it is only your own you've made.
And you need to do something visible,
you need an act you can see as a result
    of the thing in you.

> *Gerald—I told you he was my friend,*
> *Mrs. Wharton, I know this about him,*
> *just this much, but I think it is more*
> *than you have made out for yourself—he ...*
> *Gerald was attached to anyone*
> *not for what they were, but for the things*
> *they prevented ... It enabled him*
> *to give, as you call it, to give in ...*

Prevented ... You don't have your share of the robe !
    It always grows chill
in the car—February makes rides a choice
between icicles and asphyxiation.
    I feel it myself—
pull it over your knees. Ping, get off ! Don't let
    the dogs bully you :
Gerald always said they bullied me. Only
because I let them. During the last decades
of the Empire—during the Decadence, in fact—
the Emperors had a craving for human
    curiosities ;
whenever one was found, he she or it was shipped
to Rome (for they mostly came from Egypt). Once
they found a boy who understood what birds said—
now I have always been like that about dogs,
    since I was a girl :
I am a devoted animal-lover
who dislikes all animals but dogs ... Gerald

always says—said—Gerald always . . . That is true,
    he valued what kept
back the big things, and a pound of prevention
was a fortune to him. We knew the same man,
I see, if not each other. Wherever he was,
Gerald led a wife with a want at its heart . . .

> . . . *What did you say, Mrs. Wharton? Gerald led . . .*

. . . or perhaps a wound. A wanting life, or wounded;
I never guessed, he never gave me the chance
to know the difference. I waited, I worked:
where the mind burns, the moods loom, Mr. Roseman.
    I was a woman
becoming what I made, melting into print,
and those loose flames of mine fed a single fire . . .

> *At Gerald's altar? So you never*
> *learned, so busy were you tending to*
> *your . . . You never knew about Gerald.*

What I knew about Gerald I never "learned,"
    dear Mr. Roseman,
do you mean to educate me further, now?
The only corpse of any real consequence
is the one ripening—the one preparing
    itself within us.
What is there left to learn about a dead man?

> *Well, you know so much else—so many*
> *other things. Sometimes other people*
> *are right, preposterous as it seems,*
> *Mrs. Wharton, and you can learn from them.*
> *As you can when they are wrong. I am*
> *at a loss—quite happy to be there,*
> *but that is where I am, at a loss*
> *to tell if you left Teddy Wharton*
> *for literature or for Gerald . . . ?*

And whom would you tell?
Literature and Gerald were one learning,
Mr. Roseman, one gift to me—one given, if you
    must be personal.

What could be more to the point than being
personal when you are talking about
a person? Both of us knew Gerald—
I have my doubts if it was "the same man,"
as you say. For instance, he taught *you . . .*
Gerald taught me nothing. He gave me
nothing I could be said to possess.
What would be worth having? Knowledge is
not what you have but what you are . . .

And what were you, the two of you, may I ask?

As you see, we must be personal.

We must . . . not. I retract my question, Mr. Roseman.

Oh no, don't. Don't retract anything.
I see, now, it is why I am here,
why I was suggested for the job:
your question, and my answer to it.
We were what you failed to be—to become,
you and Teddy, you and Gerald: one.

Stop! Georges, arrêtez
la voiture. Il faut que les chiens sortent.
Essayez d'éviter les flaques, je ne veux pas
        qu'ils rentrent tout mouillés.
I have asked the chauffeur to walk Ping and Pong.

I understand French, Mrs. Wharton;
as you understood English, just now.

Go on, Ping, go with Georges. Mr. Roseman, I—
        I will not hear this.

You will not hear because you know "this"
already, Mrs. Wharton. How many
years has it been since Teddy died: eight?
Eight years, during which you waited for
Gerald \Mackenzie to marry you—
waited, writing in that costliest
of cabinets, the kind of life
which can be changed at any moment . . .

49

What do you know about change of life? Have you
    changed yours, Mr. Roseman?

> *It has been changed for me. Those eight years—*
> *Gerald's last and in a sense my first*
> *eight years, in which our lives overlapped—*
> *during that time of ours, Mrs. Wharton,*
> *you deluded yourself by waiting*
> *for a decision you yourself had made*
> *long since. You are, therefore you go on . . .*

So do you, Mr. Roseman, you speak with all
    the authority
of an outsider. And indeed you are one.

> *Let me go on, let me tell you this—*
> *you won't mind because I don't matter,*
> *isn't that the case? It will help you,*
> *later on, when Gerald is . . . One thing*
> *Gerald said—oh, not "always," but he said it,*
> *he said it when he knew his own mind—*
> *was that women are for men who fail.*
> *Gerald did not fail—he descended,*
> *perhaps, beneath himself in order*
> *to be on top of others, but never*
> *failed. That is why you could not figure*
> *as you expected in Gerald's life:*
> *being a woman was an abyss*
> *which might suddenly swallow you both . . .*

How would *you* know anything at all about
    being a woman?

> *I am a woman, Mrs. Wharton, for the same*
> *reason that you are a man: "self-made"*
> *at thirty-five! I am a woman just*
> *because I am a man. How could I*
> *help knowing? Besides, you help me*
> *know: you wrote books so that I would know . . .*
> *Our Gerald was not a man to think*
> *differently of a book for having*
> *read it, but I am. I read your books,*
> *and I learned what Gerald never taught*

me. Because I read your books I think
differently of life—and women.

You speak in riddles, Mr. Roseman. I don't see ...

Come now, Mrs. Wharton, you see clearly—
you see what you believe. If you are
a self-made man, you must not forget
those of us God made. What did you make
of Gerald's friends you met at Howard's—
all those appreciative listeners!
What do you make of Mr. James? Surely
you know what we are and what we do.
You may not have known the niceties—
did you visit the house in Cairo,
did you take the yacht to Syracuse,
and when Gerald was ill, were you there?
So much for what we are, what we do:
you did know that, Mrs. Wharton, didn't you?

I know what *you* are, Mr. Roseman, you tell me
            enough to know that.
Nor am I tempted to put you and Gerald
and Mr. James in the same basket of crabs
because you do—or say you did—the same things.
You are men who do not need women—that is
what you say, that is what you are telling me,
is it not? That is what you smile and tell me
            Gerald was. No need ...
One learns not to need by needing, it would seem:
            that is how I learned ...
Here are the dogs. Merci, Georges, non. Cette fois
prenez-les avec vous. Maintenant, je crois qu'ils vont
            dormir tout de suite.
Mr. Roseman, we may resume our expedition
(for such it is turning out to be, a voyage
            of discoveries)
with perhaps a different sense—with a new
dispensation of each other. You are a ...

... I have been telling you what I am,
Mrs. Wharton, so that you might not have
to say as much to me. I would spare

51

you the needless expense of . . . of
what has already been expended . . .

You call it spending!
You are, if I am correct in my assumption—
you are a Jew, Mr. Roseman, are you not?

Oh yes, Mrs. Wharton, and my father
was a banker, too—a Jew Banker!
You are correct in your assumption.
Will that make it easier for you
to realize just why I am here—
to reject your realization?
The Chosen People are commonly
treated as a people chosen for
the sake of somebody else . . . I do not
look for uncommon treatment from you,
that would hardly be fair. It is hard
for either of us to be fair now,
thanks to Mr. James . . . To be sure, I am
a Jew, you were saying, do go on . . .

I shall, Mr. Roseman.
Each of us gets—Gerald always used to say,
though doubtless not to you—the Jew he deserves . . .
When you claim I know what you are, what you do,
in that triumphant tone of yours—quite heroic—
I think you had better understand: I have
    never thought of them,
doing and *being*, as one and the same thing,
the way I thought of Gerald and literature—
    so mistakenly,
you force me to realize . . . Women, Mr. Roseman,
women defend themselves against what they are—
    that is what they *do*.
Some do it by marriage, I have defended
myself otherwise . . . too long for you to take
from me the Gerald I knew, the Gerald who
invented me—for whom I invented myself,
    if you enjoy that
way of putting it—you take Gerald from me
    and replace him with
a preposterous caricature who behaves

as people behave in the newspapers,
some newspapers, and Elizabethan plays . . .

> *Mrs. Wharton, I cannot take from you*
> *what you never had. Even Shylock*
> *could not do that. What I am saying*
> *is that Gerald led another life . . .*

There is not another life for anyone, not
      even for Gerald.
He is dead, once and for all. And for good, now.
I suppose there is another way to live . . .

> *That may be life, or what you call life,*
> *Mrs. Wharton, but it is not living—*
> *it is pretending . . . You liked Gerald*
> *to pretend, and he liked pretending.*

    Please do not go on.
To the brazen all is brass. We have nothing
in common, not even memory. Memory least of all.
    How dare you speak of
"our" Gerald as if . . . as if you had the right . . .

> *I told you I had my doubts when you,*
> *Mrs. Wharton, said we knew the same man.*
> *Certainly we have not lost the same*
> *meaning from our lives. How dare I speak?*
> *You know, Mrs. Wharton, you confirm*
> *my first impression of you, last year,*
> *as you sat there, smoking, in London,*
> *Ping on your lap, Pong at your feet—like*
> *two foxes fallen from the little*
> *wreath of dead red furs round your shoulders,*
> *with the afternoon light turning you*
> *into a sort of sibyl, circled*
> *by your own oracular vapors:*
> *I listened to you talk, and I heard*
> *all the harshness of a dogmatist*
> *mingling somehow in every sentence*
> *with the bleakness of an egoist*
> *and the pretentiousness of a snob . . .*

Is that what you heard?
So you're something of a novelist yourself—
            a novelist manqué.
How incorruptible youth is, when it has
failed to be interesting! You slash at me—
            out to draw blood now
with all the weapons in your reach, Mr. Roseman,
the mean and merciless ones which lie behind
            losses. What have you
lost? A slender man, tall, with tight skin, clear eyes,
who could not keep his hand from trembling when he
            poured a glass of wine.
Very well. I chose Gerald—you lost him.
I am quite prepared to surrender my choice:
            you still have your loss,
and you call me names for it. How do they help?
            Were you never taught
that humor is the fun we refrain from making?
What Gerald gave me was the capacity
to become independent of what he was.

            As well as of what he did, Mrs. Wharton?

            And of what he did.
I see that as well—manqué see, manqué do.
You are too young to be much interested
in a university in which we have to die;
            that is why you speak
so . . . so knowingly. I am old enough, now—
            call it middle-aged—
not to be interested in much besides.
The years are sad, the days jubilant . . .
You speak knowingly: I speak in ignorance.
            Better not to say
what you know. There might be some reason for your
knowing it. As there is for your saying it.
            One glance at the long
itinerary of our . . . relationship,
Gerald's and mine, long and wrong as it has been,
gives me the presumption of a Cassandra.

            *Yes, a Cassandra in a smart scarf
            you drape round a gray toque with that odd*

> *coquetry of yours, emphasizing*
> *your eyes until you resemble some . . .*
> *some wanderer in a wedding-veil.*

If I do wander,
it is what brings me back to you, Mr. Roseman:
    I am not a Jew,
so I wander differently from your way;
Jews—it is what I wanted to say just now . . .
    I am not so harsh
as you would have me, nor so unresourceful,
if indeed I am a sibyl, a Cassandra . . .
    Let me try once more:
Jews feel that wherever they happen to be
is home because they are there. My dear young man,
to me anywhere would seem strange that did not!
I shall try to speak as both of us deserve,
    or as Gerald does.
This is what I mean, the important detail
which escaped you in the charming genre scene
I offered and you so cleverly described:
    I am in motion.
I have all that people are valued for, but
little that could make anyone love me . . . You see,
    I have always been
everyone's admiration and no one's choice.
It is I who have done the choosing . . . Gerald—
    As I have always
done the moving. Gerald did not love me. No.
Affection and desire—those apparently
were his poles, and we divide them between us,
    you and I. We stand
for different parts of life—of Gerald's life.

> *Love, Mrs. Wharton, was in the center,*
> *somewhere—anywhere, between us two.*
> *Gerald kept it all for himself,*
> *the way trees keep shade in the desert.*
> *We have a geography of the spirit—*
> *all Americans do, even when . . .*

    . . . Even when we fail
to live up to our geography, as we have.

But as I told you before, Gerald
did not fail: in his geography
he must have had a Great Barrier Reef
of the soul, and behind it he kept
his heart—in a kind of cold storage.

Cold storage, deplorable as it may be,
     has done far less harm
to hearts than more promiscuous exposure—
than tropical mildew and dry-rot. I think
Gerald's life—or what it now appears to me
     I know of his life—
must have been lived so ... so vicariously
that only reminiscence could make it real
     to him. To me, now.

At last. So we have come to the core
of our trouble. Not that I am a Jew
or that Gerald and I took part in
those nameless sins which, when named, always
turn out to exclude the name-caller.
The trouble is that Gerald was not
the mere inspiration you believed
or were determined to believe him—
the chalk-egg that lures the hen to sit—
but a ... Mrs. Wharton, if you look past
the desolation of an empty place,
you see he was a burden to you!

To me ... ''Mere inspiration'' is a burden;
     memory, prison.
O the terrible energy of the dead!
What water falling was to Theocritus
in Sicily : nearest to the visible
     divine ... A burden!
Without the urn, the ashes I hold would weigh
     —how much, I wonder?
Gerald's death cannot define him, merely end
a life that seemed active, and even crowded,
     but ... negligible,
a kind of brilliance made up of limitations,
     my limitations,

you understand . . .
>We must be at least beyond
Ville d'Avray by now—look to the left: is that
>the spire you spoke of,
Corot's church, and Saint-Cloud lying behind it?

>>*Yes, Ville d'Avray. They call this the Bois*
>>*de Fausses Reposes. Versailles is over there . . .*

A perfect nook in which to knit a novel,
>if you can reach it!
How wretched all these banlieu thoroughfares are—
we never really escape the boundaries
of Paris, get beyond the pale . . . or the dark.

>>*The way we escape America.*

Yes. For all the drawbacks of our street-cleaning
and the excesses of our architecture,
>we do get away—
we Americans *want* to get away from
our diversions even more quickly than we
>want to get *to* them:
convenience is the tenth muse of our life . . .

>>*You speak so differently, Mrs. Wharton,*
>>*the moment you are released—relieved,*
>>*I might almost say, or I must say—*
>>*from Gerald. You become a different*
>>*woman: it is a strange mutation . . .*

>A different woman?
You cannot turn a pillar of society
into a pillar of salt without bringing
>down the synagogue.
And it is a strange journey. For me, Gerald
in the flesh was merely a preparation.
>The truth—later
the truth becomes apparent: once you regard
someone as lost to you, then he . . . only then . . .
You are never truly together with him
until he is dead and actually inside you.

57

So for you Gerald's death was simply
a kind of childbirth the wrong way round!

Nothing is "simply" ...
I told you I distrusted children, as I
distrust all victims—they win in the long run,
    if they should get one.
Born victims: children. I do not want a sense
of the past, as Mr. James keeps calling it,
    and the future is deaf—
we must not count on the future to bestow
    meaning on our acts:
if we do, all action becomes impossible.
I want a sense of the continuous life.
I—is there something wrong, Mr. Roseman?
What are you ... ? I see.
I suppose one comes to grips with grief only
by seeing it come true in others ... Take this ...

Thank you ... Mrs. Wharton, I did not
expect that. Tears are not in my line.

Nor mine, my dear man,
but I am better prepared—women must be.

You brought it all back ... Unhappiness
wonderfully aids the memory:
I was here—in Paris—with Gerald.
You remember, he escorted the heir
apparent of Siam around the Louvre ...
The prince asked no questions, never looked
right or left through all the galleries
until they stopped, and we all stopped too,
in front of some primitive Pietà.
Then his highness spoke for the first time,
asking what the group represented.
The curator of the Louvre explained,
"It is the figure of our dead God
after His enemies have crucified Him."
The prince listened, staring, but Gerald—
Gerald burst out laughing—couldn't stop,
peal after peal of awful laughter
echoing through the Louvre ... Then his face
went blank, and our procession moved on.

Do you understand, Mrs. Wharton, why
I thought of that just now? Do you know?

No, Mr. Roseman, I don't know. But I have
begun to learn something I needed to know.
    ... To learn something else.
We shall be at the cemetery before
much longer—Georges cannot take the car inside.
    They will be waiting,
the arrangements are all made—one does not leave
such matters to chance. I want to change them now.
Please!
    The urn, take it from me—
when we stop, get out and give it to the man
waiting at the grave. *I'll* wait here in the car.

You don't want to get out? You won't come?

I want you to put Gerald's ashes in the ground.
    We are, all of us,
distinctly marked to get back what we give, even
from what we may name inanimate nature.
    Take the ashes now.
When you come back, we shall decide what to say.

To say to each other, Mrs. Wharton?

    No, to Mr. James!
He has made his experiment in fiction—
    he has turned his screw,
as I suppose he would say. What shall *we* say?

I shall say nothing. People are far
more tolerant of artists, Mrs. Wharton,
than artists are of people, I find.

Silence, then, for Mr. James: it is the one
telling punishment. And for ourselves as well?
It might be premature to meet. Let us keep
    each other as last
illusions. ... Here's the drive. And here's the urn.
I leave the last of Gerald in your hands, Mr. Roseman,
    where so clearly he ...

Thank you . . . Edith, if I may. Thank you.

Thank you, Mr. Roseman.

Won't you call me by my given name?

I never heard it, I think, Mr. Roseman.

It's Gerald, Gerald Roseman, Edith.

. . . That is the first time I have laughed in a week . . .
Our story, the one we shall spare Mr. James,
is what the American public always
wants : a tragedy with a happy ending.

A silent one.

CONTRA NATURAM

for Coburn Britton

1913

    My God! Forgive me,
I had no idea this compartment was
occupied—and now I have awakened you . . .

         No, Monsieur, not now : my body wakens
         before my eyes do. I walked with you
         down the passage, I knew you were coming
         as a matter of course—*materially,*
         step by step, till you banged your way in here.
         Besides, I sleep badly enough to sleep
         again : there is no harm in waking . . .

    My apologies,
nonetheless, for what must seem an intrusion.
I take this train, this car, this compartment
    weekly, to Marseille
where I have . . . business, not that I confine—no,
yes! that is the right word, I suppose I do
have business there, commerce of a kind, Monsieur,
    but till now never
had a companion. "Commercial men" like me
will not countenance paying a first-class fare
    so short a distance.
Do not let me disturb your journey further . . .

         What does it matter ? We are almost there,
         are we not ? Was that Aix, where you got in ?

    Almost where ? Marseille ?
Yes, almost there, starting from Paris. From Aix,
    we have just begun.

How do you know I started from Paris?

Because I know you, Monsieur Rodin. Because
I find myself speaking to the one master
> *who has given, when*
so much in our moment is taken away.
And having spoken once is a tyrannous
> *reason for speaking*
again ... For me, it is a feast to find you
> *providentially*
put in my path this day ... of all days. For me
your face need not waken to be yours—I would
> *have recognized you*
years ago, known you, named you upon first sight:
my eyes, you see, wake first—I mean, before my
> *body is aware ...*

> You are not old enough to see, except
> with your eyes. That takes time, a long time. So,
> Monsieur, you know my face as well as my name.
> For you, even by accident, *providentially*,
> as you put it—whatever that may mean ...
> Never mind: for you, now, I am someone
> to "recognize" ... People come up to me,
> women on the street! I am a man without
> contemporaries, merely a public ...
> The mice of neglect, and now the vultures
> of notoriety—between them, what
> man's life is left uneaten, while he lives?
> No, that is not a question proper to
> your interests, Monsieur, not a question
> at all. What kind of business takes you—

Oh, my business never takes me out of Aix,
it is in fact none of my business to leave
> *home, Monsieur, rather*
my "commercial" folly. But to find you here ...
> *It is reported*
(though evidently an exaggeration)
that you never leave your residence, that you
entertain the world on your terms at Meudon,
> *one sanctuary*
where you have some security against us,

against such devouring tribute as these
    recognition-scenes . . .
I would not, for the world, seem predatory,
and yet I must not fail this great occasion
    for my gratitude—

        Gratitude, Monsieur, for the work I do?
        It is for what I will do yet, the work
        to come, that I shall need your gratitude.

   And you shall have it,
without fail. Why once, in fact, visiting **Paris,**
I waited at the gateway, Rue de Varenne,
but lost my courage when I saw your studio . . .

        My studio! The moment those Cambodians
        took over Meudon, what could I call mine?

   Those Cambodians?

        The Khmer dancers, here with **King Sisowath.**
        One week with them and there was only chaos—
        the kind of disorder *critics* would call
        a landscape if it happened to be outdoors . . .
        Not like yours, Monsieur—you are from Aix,
                you said?—
        your mountains that rise from the plain
                as though
        well rested, your aqueduct that makes even
        water into a good citizen . . . I mean
        ruins, what those children did to my things,
        "my" studio. And yet—would you
                believe it?—
        I cannot bear the place without them now,
        reminded by dozens of my own drawings
        what it was to live in the habitude
        of sumptuous forms—reminded by no more
        than a gathering of tender wreckage
        what Antiquity has to give . . . Gone now,
        they have been gone one day . . . One day
                between
        their genius for disarray and *that,* Monsieur,
        that rational landscape of yours out there,

                63

is as long as a day out of Genesis!
I congratulate you upon your luck,
finding them at your own doorstep, nearly—
you have a sense of occasion, perhaps
that is what you meant by *providence*,
though it will be our mutual forfeit . . .
You plan to see them in Marseille tonight
before they sail back into their own past?

Them—who? Oh, I see,
the Cambodian dancers. No, I shall not
see them—I do not come to Marseille for that . . .
for such attractions . . .
I may have, Monsieur, a sense of occasion,
as you so kindly say, but has not each one
of the senses its own particular eunuch?
I do not live among
"forms" in an office, a room, a café,
and I must therefore find them, must search them out,
my sumptuous forms . . .
They visited you at Meudon, Monsieur Rodin,
these Orientals—and their proximity
stimulated you?

Stimulated? They have ruined my life!
Nothing I recognize remains in place.
You know the Cathedral of Rouen? Last
Sunday I went off to Rouen (it takes
a whole cathedral to put me in my
place, to bring me to my senses) : well,
Monsieur, the very stones of Rouen under
my hands were no better than a myth,
a memory, more likely a mistake . . .
But let one of those golden Khmers reveal
that nakedness before me, moving past
the others like parts of a broken vase—
fragments that remember being of earth—
and there is nothing else real in the world!
I feel myself slowly, inevitably
flowing toward death : a defense of darkness
fell around those bodies—except that they
glowed with an incommunicable light . . .
A fall comes only to those capable

of a creation, must it not be so?
With them, you see, I collaborated
in the absent cathedral. Now, of course,
I pursue them for my last look, even
in a theatre where I can only look . . .

Only! Only look . . .
Yet you are a man whose glance is obeyed. How
privileged you are, looking . . . How available
*   the relation of*
what you choose to see, Monsieur, and what you choose!
Does not the eye, altering, alter all? I—

You do not follow me, Monsieur. A man
in private is a man, and in public
he is . . . in public. Merely that. Nothing
cures me of my pleasures, my desires, call them
that, like compromising them in public.

You want *to be cured*
of desire, Monsieur Rodin—as of a disease?
You think it is a sickness, this need to look?

I am seventy-two years old, Monsieur.
If I must renounce desire, it will be
out of respect—for fear I do it some
disgrace. But I shall not turn against it.
Growing older, I have grown defiant
of "my" limbs, "my" body, "my" face—
                              the things
that are mine have become suspect. I have
reverence enough for desire to renounce it
before it has fled me altogether . . . You see,
I have had a revelation from these
wordless muses. They remind me: pleasure
is unknown to almost everyone, for lack
of lightness—lightness which does not cancel
gravity, but conditions grace. Pleasure
at this pitch transforms us, it is a kind
of alchemy, a metamorphosis
we undergo without scandal because
we have only a spectre for witness.

65

These children—I cannot make one out from
another, they are a slither of flesh . . .

And they? Can they make
you out from another man—make you out from me,
for instance, Monsieur Rodin? Do they know you?

No, for once there is no fear of being
recognized for myself in that behavior
of theirs, that fugitive delirium
which signifies the passage of the god . . .
Monsieur, they are children, they look to me
girls of thirteen, who cannot speak one word
of French! Perhaps they cannot speak at all . . .

Girls? Are there no
boys in the troupe? But it is no matter, their
silence is golden . . .

Theirs is a silence which has more to do
with adoration than with sensuality . . .
We come to our senses and resume worship
of the god. I tell you—I am trying
to tell you: desire does without a face—
it makes do, and leaves us without "ourselves."

Monsieur, you tell me
what I know: friendship and love, they are ourselves
when we are, friendship and love are someone:
desire is anyone.

Anyone else. I called it an alchemy, Monsieur:
the practice of certain pleasures changes
the body into a strange basilisk,
a dragon always female—and always sacred,
reverent. Unmixed attention is prayer.

Female! You say it,
Monsieur Rodin, and I can believe you, yet
I cannot always—I take you sometimes in my
stumble, not my stride.
Why is the body you speak of as a dragon
always female?

The deepest experience of a maker
is female, Monsieur, the experience
of receiving and bearing—it begins
in an attempt to make appearance real,
and ends, if it can end, in an attempt
to make reality appear. That is
what I mean by a female experience . . .

It has not been mine—I misunderstood you,
Monsieur Rodin. But I am not a maker,
merely a man. And my deepest, my dearest
    experiences—

Are not with girls. Is that not the case?

    It is the case. It
is what I have to thank you for, Monsieur Rodin.
You have been, from the first, the inspiration
of us all—I mean, nothing is true for all
of us, if it is not first true for one . . . You are
    that one, you have dared
to give a body to the man we call, or
    have been taught to call
the god in man. If we believe anything
passionately enough, it turns to something else;
    it has turned for me . . .
Do you know where I go, on these weekly jaunts?
    I can tell you now
with equanimity, bare my disgrace to you
    as if it were pride:
I go, Monsieur, to the baths, to "haunts of vice,"
the places where men give themselves up to each
other, where they give themselves up . . . Surrender . . .
    There each of us is
universal but not individual—and there
    I go precisely
to be haunted: it is neither Jacques nor Jean
I look at, once they are naked before me,
    but Endymion
who stands, momentarily illuminated
    in a clearing, dim
as moonlight, where the intermediaries—

poor shivering sweating human flesh—are there
    as a substitute,
and where touch itself is a futility,
for these bodies are no more than allusions
    to the sole Presence
of the god. Ever since your first work, ever
    since "The Age of Bronze"—

Why must you add me to your lineage?
Surely *my* line of descent is clear, from
Praxiteles to Michelangelo
and then Rodin. I have no part in yours . . .

But you have given me evidence, Monsieur,
how deeply you participate in my delight,
    if not my desire . . .
In all your work I know, pleasure rises to
    the pitch of vision,
so that what separates one mouth from the rest
is no more than a missed opportunity . . .
It is your gift, the courage of all my hours
    watching the young men—
they come off their ships, come, I have no doubt,
to be watched . . . Perhaps certain postures, certain
attitudes of pleasure, just because they are
    intolerable
to reason, incompatible with dignity,
generate an innocence that is their own . . .
    No, I do not seek,
Monsieur, the intimacy of a mutual
    embarrassment, not
for the world would I attempt to coerce . . .

Embarrassed? I am not so ready as
you suppose me, Monsieur, to admit
complicity with your . . . pleasures. Let us
abstain from such charges. Grant that I am
not innocent of them because I am not
guilty of them. There is no more to say.
I do not condemn, nor do I condone.

And yet, last month only, I was told—I read
somewhere, perhaps, of Nijinsky's visit to you . . .

We are all at the mercy of gossip—
invisible ink. You are misinformed.
I shall tell you what occurred: far better
the tale should have a decent burial
than a mocking perpetuation. Last
month—you are right about that—before these
Khmer interruptions, these interferences . . .
Modern life is not simple, nor should it be:
it is not for nothing we are heirs to
the ages. So you have heard of Nijinsky,
Monsieur, the great Russian faun . . . It is true,
he had come to Meudon, had come to pose.
I modelled him all that day, that morning
on the terrace: he danced for me there, back
and forth, moving without music, without
motivation, it would seem, far too much
a child of the universe to be a man
of the world—stood still long enough (the

                    young

are often temporary artists) for me
to observe how nature constructs her solids
out of her liquids . . . To observe, Monsieur,
the identity of the evanescent
with the enduring. You can imagine . . .

    I can. I know why
we like to watch the sexual: to observe,
Monsieur, the identity of fulfilment
with renunciation. It is reality . . .

By noon, reality had exhausted me,
and the boy as well. Wine was brought

               outside—

after all, our disorders have always been
a part of our riches—and we drank, too much
perhaps for the pair of us, old and young,
in the sunshine, under my terrace wall,
and fell asleep, I suppose: I remember
an unguarded hour, the sunlight, the weight
of the boy's head against my hip, and then
the suddenness of its removal when
he leaped up. In the doorway stood—no,

                 loomed

69

an enormous black bear, a Russian bear
pointing at me, me! and screeching
                    "pédéraste!

pédéraste!" Serge de Diaghilev had come
to claim his property, which he believed
I had thought to rob him of. I have had
many thoughts since that day, Monsieur, many
questions . . . I cannot imagine myself—

Nor need you. Certain
efforts of the body submit the soul, or
expose it, to strange commitments, Monsieur Rodin.
At such moments, what countenance could it take,
        it is well to ask . . .
The salt of the earth and the sweet of the earth,
        are they not one thing?

The soul, Monsieur! The body is the soul!
Doubtless, at such "moments," as you call
                                        them,
it turns away, feigning absence. Ecstasy
is always a danger. It should always
have just happened—not be in the present.
I do not share, nor do I want to share
your preferences, though I do not go
so far as to call them vices. For me
some vices are so . . . so unnatural
they do not exist. I do not judge you . . .

Judge, Monsieur Rodin!
If we are judged, it will not be for the silly
transgression of failing to appreciate
        others, it will be
for the supreme transgression of failing
to appreciate ourselves, as I believe
        you fail, may I say?

What is the failure you accuse me of?

I am a man, speaking
to a man: I cannot tell you everything.
Some harmonies can prevail only over
        a heap of ruins.

You must be a schoolteacher, Monsieur, or
at the very least an auctioneer:
it is irresistible, I confess
I find it so, the way you give yourself out . . .

Irresistible
still more, the way you keep yourself in, the way
you conceal . . . Perhaps you will accompany me
when we reach Marseille—I see we are nearly . . .

When we reach Marseille, you will join *me,*
Monsieur, for a meal perhaps before we
visit those dancers of mine—or of ours?

No, Monsieur, I shall go to my filthy haunts—
I shall not invite you again to join me there.
Our moment has been
a history only of departed things
or a mere fiction of what never was.
You need not join me—
we are joined, Monsieur. I hope you see it now . . .

It is not what I see, but what I see by
that matters. We shall not meet again.

But we have met now.
Nor can I determine if the miseries
of continued possession are less dreadful
than the struggles of continued exorcism.
Let us call a truce . . .

I shall do you the honor to forget
all that you have told me this afternoon.
Well met, Monsieur, and parted well. Adieu.

Adieu, Monsieur Rodin.

A NATURAL DEATH

for Françoise Choay

Summer, 1947

I

Pesaro.   Professor Hemming, I am in the wrong
   period! None of which is left now. Only
     what came before or will come next
        remains to be seen.
There has been no *rapido* from Rimini
   since the War; a bus lets you off (you
     and the pigs and hens) at noon.
Noon in Pesaro,
     do you know what that means? a yellow
       darkness to illustrate all
         shadows—not darkness,
           not yellow either:
       a light that shows up
     every pimple on your skin,
   but not one color of the spectrum.
I just made it to
   San Domenico (1390), and came out blinder
     than the bats inside. A sacristan
       drew me a map, though he *dreads*
         all Americans
(we bombed the Foglia bridge) : lucky for me the Villa
   is on this side. Of course I would have to walk.
       I walked, on what they call a *spiaggia,*
the lunatic fringe
   of the sea, polluted with green leather froth;
     the snakes drop into it as you pass—
       they look like arrows swimming,
         even wickeder
     than on land, if that hot slime *is* land.

It will be worth it, I thought,
                slithering past them
(though all I could see
                was boxes, inland,
        piled up there by cave-dwellers
    who could not find a cliff)—worth it all
                to reach my first real
Sandro di Fiore : not a sketch, a blueprint,
    But the Thing Itself, on the Villa
            grounds, the great Scena Marina ...
                Professor Hemming,
there was no path, no signpost : I had to jump across
    cracks in the dry ground, as if the earth had split
        open like a dead pomegranate.
Sand shot up in shrouds,
        then fell back. Suddenly nine birds went
            over, like one triangular piece
                of metal trembling only
                    around the edges.
    I am not a coward, you know that,
        and a girl who's on her own
                in Italy learns
to put up with things.
                But these were not things !
                These were ... omens—ominous.
        Still, I kept on, until the Villa
                came in sight, by five,
    and though the dazzle on the water was not
    so needle-sharp, the stored-up staleness
            of the day simmered round me,
                sour, blistering, dumb.
Sforza built the Villa, Dossi frescoed it, later
        (1493) Lucretia Borgia poisoned someone here.
            And in the park, my poor lost *Maestro*
was allowed to make
    his Sea-Theatre, sixty-three years ago.
        Sforza ... Borgia ... Delle Rovere ...
            Their stones still stand, for them Time
                is at a standstill,
        their heartless marble persons beckon
            and their history begins.
                This place makes you want

to have old lovers
        back, old victories,
      good things you may have done once.
   They do not seem to matter here, where
       nothing matters past
  the past. I took the wrong hero then, the wrong
    Alessandro. Is that why nothing
      is left? There was the Scena,
        made too late to last:
not Renaissance but wrecked, whitewash graying in salt air,
   oleanders growing out of what had been a wall—
    I just don't see what could have been *done*
in this ... this refuse.
    Sandro said: Realism was just exposure;
      Art, revelation. What was revealed
       inside these palings, what shown
        in this arena
          dumped out of daylight
      by a clump of stakes,
     where all Mystery shrivels
   from the malice of comparison?
Professor Hemming,
   one last hiss upon the living shore, and then
     the sea died out (when it is warmer
      than marble, it looks somewhat
        harder). In this world,
God only and the Angels may be spectators. We
   have our work to do. *Theatre of the sea!*
    I left the recent ruin to the tide—
short work, I should say.
    Next time you hear, it will be from Bussaco,
     where I hope Di Fiore and I have
      better luck. *Best,* CYNTHIA.

II

Bussaco.   Your letter, Professor Hemming, was here
   waiting for me. Wonderful news or fond hopes?
    I wonder. With each "new" building lost,
      is Fiore living

more likely to make good such losses to me
than Fiore dead—drawings and gossip?
Remember that interview
with Victor Horta:
advantages of leaving off leaves
and flowers both, retaining
nothing but the stem!
Sandro saying: "Sap
is the grammar of all
ornament," and Horta kicking
Sandro's cane and asking: "Does it still run through *that?*"
I can imagine
how you must be cringing at the chapter now—
"Fallacies of Organic Theory . . ."
Having no stone to turn to,
hearsay is a help,
Professor Hemming—what can you do with nothing but
the truth? If our old man is alive, I know
I must sound him out, and I will, but
"life" gets in the way.
There is enough on record, and wrecks enough,
as I began to write you: The room
they gave me in Coimbra makes
any *Spanish* inn,
for all they say, seem like the Statler.
Again I had to walk, ten
blank kilometers
to where Bussaco
begins. Like a wall
the woods rise against you, cork
and Lusitanian oak, laurustine,
giant arbutus,
and what they call maritime fir. No sunlight
gets down to you—nothing but trunks, boles,
saplings plastered together,
endless erections—
what else could you call them? In 1622 Pope Gregory
prohibited women from entering the woods.
It makes enchanted ground, thousands
of acres of it,
a kind of male Mystery Cult, those trees up
and up, and no hope of lying down;

even the dead trees stand up
against each other,
propped on the living ones, no falling
here except for water, springs
suddenly making
the dark columns loud.
And at the center,
Sandro's huge folly, erected
for the queer count who never got there—
assassinated
—and forgotten, like him, since 1914.
You know how *I* got there? A white dog
ran past me with a white bone
in its mouth: a sign.
I followed. It is an easy step to take, calling
something divine because it cannot speak.
Anyway, I followed and I came
to what might have been
Sleeping Beauty's castle house before the Prince.
I stood there staring—all I could do
was stare at what had turned into
a single treetrunk—
of course it was streaked and stained with vines
that hung like so many shawls
but could not hide it:
Fiore's hunting lodge!
a whited sepulchre,
dead white, nothing to see there
but another part of the forest
gone to its white end.
The first death is red, then black, the white one last:
white things are always an afterthought,
doubles or seconds of real things,
parodies of them,
like that mad White Mass conducted by time and darkness
before my eyes. I'll never know what Sandro
had in his mind (nor am I so sure
Sandro had a mind):
not hunting, that I *am* sure of, and—God knows—
no lodging here. Professor Hemming,
I am sick and tired. Of course
it was easier
getting out of that

phallic labyrinth
than getting in, but what is
the good of it all, going on to Var—
even if the church
is really there, for once, not washed out to sea,
or victimized by vegetable
penis envy ? I suppose
the good is getting
onward and upward
to Bloemenwerf, one building
famous enough even for Flemings
to preserve. Grant me this : never has a research
fellowship been harder earned. If he is alive,
I guess I'll have to tell *il Maestro*
what is left of him :
I don't know whether to extend sympathy
or spank him for what I've been through.
I'll decide between here and
France. *Best,* CYNTHIA.

III

Les Gorges du Céans (Corniche du Var). Professor Hemming,
I cannot wait, although our letters will cross,
most likely : I hope mine reaches you
in a proper state,
before it is quite wizened and must be steeped
in water like anemones from Grasse.
The fact is ... No, sentences
starting with such words
are always lies. Not fact but *finding*
is why I must write : I came
across the red corniche
(summer service of
La Compagnie du Ski—
a private railroad-car is not
an acquired taste : one takes to it then
and there, straight from Nice),
expecting another of Fiore's dead secrets
confided to the public and very

faithfully kept, but instead
I can see it now,
actually there! preposterous pillars and cones
of the Chapel Penitent, thousands of feet
above my window-sill, but in sight!
And it is a sight—
ten fingers of the earth, imploring stone, hands—
the strange and still religious nightmare
from which there is no waking
save in sleep. The prince
died from the bite of his pet monkey
and was succeeded by his father,
King Alexander,
who was mad enough
and nearly rich enough
to let Fiore turn the world
back to Will. It looks that way from here,
as if everything
possessed the power to transform itself, or else
be transformed. Professor Hemming, you
were right after all, thank God!
I'm going up there
with my camera now, and a man to take the measurements.
What the money of a guilty Balkan king
and the genius (it *was* genius, yes)
of Alessandro
managed to make, will be the making of my
dissertation, as you foresaw. More
tonight, once down. *A bientôt* . . .

Your letter was here when I got back.
Professor Hemming, *got back*
from what? From chaos,
nothing but stones, sweating grooves, lizards, lumps of a cliff
populous with ravens that kept crying out,
ravening obscenities, no doubt—
tragedia buffa!
Not penitence but dissolution, no trace
of the shaping spirit, no index
of a man's hand. Amazing,
to have your letter

to come back to then, counselling hope
hard upon that blind grotto—
grotesque!—out of which
the hot wind whistled,
as if to keep up
its spirits. "There is no joy
in the world but the joy we have *had*,"
you write, "the only
issue is by forfeiture, by *losing* something."
Professor Hemming, I can renounce
what I never had, but could he,
can he, at ninety-four?
A miracle, you call it, Fiore's being alive
(more of one, I think, your finding out
where he has gone to earth)—but can I
meet a miracle
on its own ground, disclosing to an old man
who once said "Never copy the old
but never forget the old"
that he no longer
exists, everything
gone? Surely you see
a somewhat rusty irony
in telling me first to ferret out
Fiore where he lies,
and then that the Bloemenwerf Town Hall was bombed
by *both* the Luftwaffe and the R.A.F.—
the one public edifice
up in flames, or down
in ashes, casualties of war quite casually
disposed of. Dear Professor Hemming,
I'll go to Paris, Rue Guénégaud,
but I will not give
the word to Fiore—I can ask what he *meant*,
not what they *mean*, and I can record
his answers. No more—enough.
Fondly, CYNTHIA.

I V

Paris.   In order to tell you anything at all
   I must tell you all in order. Taking life
      as it comes, what it comes to is this:
                     things we never get
      over. I will *send* over my saga now,
         and together we can sort it out
         later—like Thea and Tesman.
Tonight then let me
   simply translate, transcribe, temporize
      and testify . . . It is hard
         to live up to our
                     daily disasters
         and fatal not to.
      The Rue Guénégaud is dim,
   dirty, and so dull you cannot tell
anything about it
   but the truth. Behind her pane, a concierge screamed
      faint instructions like a boiled ghost
         whispering invective—six
                     stories to Fiore,
whose door was opened by a string tied to the bedpost,
   and in the bed lay an ancient man who looked
      exhausted by his own head of hair:
white hair gray with dirt,
   yellow with age, and eyebrows that were the skins
      of some small mammal just not large enough
         to be used as mats. My *pneu*
                     was lying open
      where someone had left it (not his nurse!
         Nursing he called ‘‘a tribute paid
            to sexuality
by those who object
         to the usual means’’)
      and where *he* left his . . . what?
   When I think of his dinners and how
                  he ate, I wonder
he and his cats were not sick together every day
   for their dessert! All that dingy afternoon
      he would smile into my staring face
            with an amiable

awareness I was there, and yet with a sort of absence :
   I was all there for him—he was not all there
     for me. I took it down, every word
(*that* much was all there)
   in Gregg for which I am forever grateful,
    having shown since highschool a certain
     idiot flair—though I know, now,
        why it is we call
  our tyrants *dictators*. I asked him, first,
     if he had written memoirs
      of a life so long
  by any measurement,
      even by shadows.
     The voice that answered verged on
    a rustle, the sound of cloth ripping
      or water running—
  some incessant impulse nearly audible
   in the next arrondissement :

I never wanted to remember   if I did I might keep the future
from happening   the past encroaches   each hour is made new
by forgetting yesterday   forgetting   there is no difference
between being no longer   and never having been   what
matters is to come widowed to our joys   I am proud of what I
am not what I have done   was it all to end in a counting-house
on top of a cinder-heap   memoirs   in the world of memory
we do not see things splendid as they are   we see nothing   I
have not lived in my time I have lived through it   there is a
choice in this world   we must choose between time and eternity
what you make is only the means of disowning the past   and
of course as you will learn my dear once you disown the past
you have no defence against the future

        that was
     when I could ask (for I had
       no heart to *tell* him)
   about the dismembered sites : Pesaro, Bussaco, Var.
    "Not what you remember, then, but what you meant,
     what you had in mind when you made it—
  a building . . . a place
   like the Sea-Theatre ?"

in mind child   I had nothing in mind   it was in the body I

had it in the body I made it to be inimitable like the sea closing
even as it opens   leaving no trace   I'll tell you how it was
D'Annunzio took me on a yacht   there were islands in the mist
'now watch that one' he told me and ordered a cannon to be
fired   he was always firing firing   gulls by the thousands
mounted like veils from the island up into the sky   circling
overhead   and calling calling   that was my Scena Marina
child   I did not make it for the mind   nor has the body fallen
as pious people suggest so much farther than the soul   I
wanted to make one dance there one dance of arms white arms
the rest darkness and out of that the voices accompanied by
arms   life itself passing like the weaver's shuttle in and out of
that wonderful web of women   the white moments of life   I
could not make them do it   my theatre sank into a vortex of
jealousy   fraud and falsehood   there will always be insanity
in the average   average women who wanted to succeed
success   whenever I came near it near success the more beauty
I saw in what is called failure   failure is not in the nature of
things   failure is the nature of things

Professor Hemming
that sounded like my cue: "the nature
of things"—and Fiore sounded
in a telling vein.
I said I had been
to Bussaco, and just the name was needle enough:
I had struck an artery!

you went there   you saw it you saw Bussaco   well of course
that was not life   that was not a theatre   that was a tryst
another thing   my dear would you hand me that   no there the
bedpan I suppose you would call it love   when the Count
mentioned what he wanted a hunting lodge it sounded like an
offer of the last straw   but that was only his pretext his
prevarication   he wanted a place in the forest where he met
his passions that was his name for them   a man with the
expression of a collie-dog into which has entered the soul of
Casanova   and I gave him love I gave him   there in the
heart of Broceliande you have been to the forest you saw it
here my child would you take this down the hall   the last door
you will see the place   I gave him passion you know the
story of Pelléas and Mélisande my dear I see that you know
everything   you found it   and the part in the story where

Pelléas stands at the tower it is in the third act   he cannot
reach her and she cannot reach him they strain to touch one
another and then Mélisande leans down out of the broken tower
and she lets down her hair   it is a kind of rapture a terrible
rapture and Pelléas stands inside Mélisande's hair that is what
I made for him I let the Count stand   even alone   even by
daylight inside Mélisande's hair   I wanted to show him I
wanted him to find out what comes of 'passion' when the will
is not frustrated but extinct   when there is no cause and no
consequence when there is only the moment and the moment
brings   not terror but freedom   freedom from memory   I
knew it the instant my design was done we are all deluded
like Mélisande by our innocence   and we are all corrupted like
Golaud by our experience   there is only relinquishment   my
dear girl the most poetical thing in the world is not being
sick   we are suspended between nature and nothingness in
that place where we have the truth of our bodies   it is not
poetic   it is the truth   only truth can be exaggerated   nothing
else will stand the strain   as I became an older man I became
a newer artist   and the end of art my dear you know what
that is the end of art   it is the recovery of paradise   when
the Count took holy orders I decided to go off to Aleppo and
give up art too   art seemed to me to be full of regrets whereas
Aleppo is only full of fleas   but I did not go   you have to
entertain the pang and taste the bitterness for all they are
worth   you have to know what has happened to you

imagine,
what it must have been like, then,
knowing what I knew,
hearing (listening
at least, for I was
writing much too fast to hear)
imagine my despair knowing I would have
to tell him the truth!
Not until I had made him talk about Var,
not until then, I resolved, and asked—
had he ever revisited his
Chapel Penitent
since its construction?

I never go back   I do not want to see them again   they have
existed   the undiscovered regions of art Fuseli says are

dreams   when I look for existence I look for it in myself
the sands drift in   the buildings are rmembered   that life
never lets go   nor do you want it to   it is part of this
room this bed   its towers and domes are the architecture of
these bedclothes   the dead   we are always debtors to the
dead   we feel they have not had their chance   that is what
the King felt   as if life had given us unfair advantages
he tried all the mediums   voices squeaking   where the missing
collar-stud has been for thirty years   the passionate dead
act within us   they are not messenger-boys and hotel-porters
even Alexander found it so   the dead who really live   the dead
whose presence we know we hardly care to call back or even
speak of   that was what I could give him   you know how a
Greek woman's dress was rinsed in brine and then pulled
lengthwise and slowly twisted until it looked like a bundle
of knots   when it was dry and the knots were loosened it had
the secret of clinging to the body   every limb revealed forever
that was the garment I made for the body of this death   I
made it of stone   and when the King came to Var he knew it
he recognized it   my dear you are forever asking what I meant
what I mean   you tell me you were there and you saw it why do
you ask for meaning   I never put two stones together to mean
anything   for a while at first meaning simplifies and then it
supersedes the world   when Alexander came to Céans I was
telling you he looked up to the chapel at the top of the gorge
and he gave one great cry 'leave me with my dead' he moaned
and that was all   reality becomes perceptible child only for
the man who accepts death it is not a thing you can learn
how could you my dear you keep writing with all the
self-assurance of a duchess writing writing   a duchess with
two lovers

It was always duchesses,
kings, and counts for Di Fiore—
those were the terms he employed,
for *they* employed him.
Perhaps that gave me the notion, Professor **Hemming**;
I was at a loss again, but I wanted
to give him something, comfort him
for all those losses
he did not even know he had suffered yet.
I wanted to thank him for being
alive, and I gave
what I had to give:

84

an *Aureus* of Hadrian,
a phoenix on the reverse,
a coin I've carried since I was in school.
He could not see it
for himsef, and when I told him what it was
his withered fingers were caressing,
I thought he would fling it at me!
Something in his face
faltered then, but his voice did not falter,
and if his mind dismantled a little,
he could master it:

this is a Roman coin   Rome of the Antonines   it is the
reign of the Beast competing accounting ruling remembering
under Rome a man could endure anything without virtue not
this   do not give me this   it is the past   it is all I have
ever opposed you have seen my buildings you know my work
she read me your letter   you know what I have done it is
beatitude of creatures I 'meant' the processes of plants
not this money not this death   I merely discovered an old
secret   the past need not exist   life can be lived without
the history of itself   or it cannot perhaps   who said life
was to be lived   endured   no ecstasy endures it grows and
it dies out   not this order not this coin it is no currency
it does not move or change   I do not serve the law   it is
not history or even knowledge but a kind of incoherent
gratitude   no purpose but ecstasy   art must go out   take it
back my dear   take it away from me it is not the earth only
history

Not once, I think, in all the dismay
of that dreadful downward wake—
the Sea-Theatre
dissolved at Pesaro,
the Lodge overgrown
at Bussaco, the Town Hall
in cinders at Bloemenwerf, at Var
the Chapel stone dead—
not once, Professor Hemming, had I lost heart
or hope of recovering Fiore
from himself, till he returned
my coin that had been   ·
a talisman for me, a sign I was keeping faith

85

with all we have been, with all we might have been.
I heard my own words before I knew
I had spoken them:
"*Maestro*, I did not mean to disappoint you.
I did not mean to tell you at all,
but you say you want to know ...
And now that *I* know
what your expectations are, perhaps
I can give you satisfaction.
They are no longer
what you made them to be.
they are no longer.
That is why I have troubled you
for meanings." And I told all of it,
what I had found there,
or not found, in Pesaro, Bussaco, Var,
and what your letter consigned to fire
as well—for the price of one
miserable coin
I spent Fiore's lifework as I might have spilled
his chamberpot. Professor Hemming, if I was
hurt and then humbled by my own spite,
I think I was *horrified*
by what happened then:
the old man took hold
of that ridiculous string
until he could grasp the bedpost,
grimaced a little
but rose up, bolt upright now, until his eyes
—cloudy, colorless, a statue's eyes—
stared into mine, and a chill
or charge or tremor
ran through what must have been all the bare bones
(and only bones) under the nightshirt,
even his hair shook ...
Then it all ended, and Fiore was speaking,
though the figure in front of me seemed.
to have no connection with
the words I was hearing, the words he must have spoken!

they are gone then   gone now   irrecoverable as a sunset
when there is no triumph to show then night becomes the
triumph   darkness purposeless   it has come   and I was right
to come here   why do you suppose I chose Paris   dying

slowly here of hand-to-mouth disease   there was no road until
I took this road   every great city has twelve-hundred
inhabitants   Paris is the sole exception   Paris has not twelve-
hundred but one-hundred-twenty   I came here to be found   I
leave the rest where they lie   or had I better say where they
fell   it is only when you have   given everything that you can
give more   that you have more to give   it is inadmissible
for a man to leave   the trace of his passage upon earth   give
it all back   the elements   the compassionate sea   and the fire
and the ground   and the growing air   as you described it
we must survive what we have made   it is not ours   I have
survived in Paris   my body separates me   nothing more than
that and an indefinable fragrance of perpetual female
possession   I waited for you   and I can wait for you no longer
my dear because you have arrived   a phoenix on the reverse
easier to love than to mourn

I know he was still
looking into my eyes, I know he was
still alive then, for the change
began there : *his* eyes
filled and overflowed,
his body fell away—only it did not fall,
it faded out, until I could not see
the little landslide of bones
under the bedclothes.
The head rolled over
and the face was gone. Even
the hands were erased. I was alone.
Professor Hemming,
that was the death of Alessandro di Fiore,
and I think I brought it to him.
I think he waited for me
to bring him that death.
It is not what I came to do, half-way across
Europe, it is not what I meant to do,
but it is what I have done. Destroyed
or delivered him—
I don't know which. I need the distance,
I need time. I need your help.
I send you all this :
please keep it for me
until it becomes
mine. *Yours,* CYNTHIA.

RICHARD HOWARD

*Richard Howard was born and educated
in Cleveland, Ohio, and studied at
Columbia University and the Sorbonne.
He is a distinguished translator from
the French and a critic of great
versatility. His four earlier books of
poems are* QUANTITIES *(1962),* THE
DAMAGES *(1967),* UNTITLED SUBJECTS
(1969), and FINDINGS *(1971); he is the
author of* ALONE WITH AMERICA: Essays
on the Art of Poetry in the United States
since 1950, *and of the commentary in*
PREFERENCES, *a recent critical anthology
of the relations between fifty-one
contemporary poets and the poetry of
the past.*

PS
3558
08826 Two-part inventions
T9
1974

Howard, Richard.

DATE			